AF540562

Tribals in Transition

TRIBALS IN TRANSITION

Edited by

DR. S. N. TRIPATHY
Dept. of Economics,
ASKA Science College,
Aska (Orissa)

1999
DISCOVERY PUBLISHING HOUSE
NEW DELHI-110 002

First Published-1999

ISBN 81-7141-482-6

Published by:
DISCOVERY PUBLISHING HOUSE
4831/24, Ansari Road, Prahlad Street,
Daryaganj, New Delhi-110 002 (*INDIA*)
Phone: 3279245
Fax: 91-11-3253475

Printed at:
Arora Offset Press,
Delhi-110092.

Preface

Ours is a large country, unique in its diversity of nature and people. In our country, known for the extreme poverty of the masses, the tribals constitute the core of the poor. Poverty, poor health and sanitation, illiteracy and other social problems among the tribals, are exerting a dragging effect on the Indian economy. The tribals survived on their skills and bartering of minor forest produce and their handicrafts to the middlemen in the garb of money lenders, who exploit them. Therefore, a development strategy will be considered successful, if it touches the problem of tribals. During five year plans, continuous efforts have been made to uplift the tribals and to reduce their poverty in our country. The Five Year Plans formulated for implementation series of investments—backed schemes and projects for the betterment of the conditions of the tribals living in the rural and urban areas. Such projects and schemes are too many to recount them here. Some benefits and advantages did reach the tribal households living in the towns. However, they are largely belonging to the land owning groups (including that of the tribals). The landless have remained without any tangible benefits and hence, deprived of the opportunities of progressive change in their life and lifestyle. Of course, in Kerala or West Bengal, the landless received support from the political organisations and their movement for upward social mobility. But in the state like Gujarat the Political agitational groups did not keep to alter the conditions of the landless tribals, though other tribals like Dhodias, Gamits and Choudharis did benefit somewhat by the tenancy acts.

Many of the tribes with their forest-dwelling culture did not have the motivation or the skill of settled cultivation. As a result, their land has been alienated to their better endowed tribal neighbours or non-tribals.

Orissa is one of the most fascinating ethnographic state of India. It has been the home of as many as 62 different tribal communities along which the Kondh top the list in numerical preponderance. The word Kondh is supposed to have been derived from Telugu word 'Kanda' which means hill. The Kondhas are thickly populated in the districts of Koraput, Phulbani and Kalahandi of Orissa.

Broadly the Kandhas are divided into three groups :

(i) The Kutia Kondhs are the weakest section of the Kandh community leading an isolated life of poverty and backwardness.

(ii) The Dangria Kondhas are comparatively less primitive in horticulture.

(iii) The desia Kandha have left the hills and forest and settled down in plains. They have chosen agriculture as the means of their livelihood.

The agency area in Orissa is predominantly inhabited by the Kutia Kandha which is one of the major sections of the Kondh tribe. Kutia Kandhas are primitive tribes living in the top of Belghar hill (Phulbani District, Orissa) situated at a height of more than 2000ft. above the sea level.

The tribal development experiences of the last 48 years suggest that in spite of all intervention programmes, the Kutias of Phulbani (Orissa) still continues to be in the grip of under development, indebtedness, misery and deprivation.

It has been observed that the growing corruption at all levels of public investments, leakages of funds, apathy of the implementing and administrative personnels imposition of plants from above, unawareness of tribals about the plans and developmental schemes have resulted in failure of plans to ameliorate their socio-economic problems. Thus, it has been observed that the developmental measures launched so far have not benefited the tribals to the extent they were contemplated; at their initiation. The post independence phase witnessed the incorporations of the provisions for the safeguard of the tribals in the Indian Constitution along with the developmental measures like tribal sub-plan, flow of institutional credit, etc., for ameliorating their socio-economic conditions.

The gamut of legislative safeguards for tribals spans for 48 years, the main landmarks being the constitutional provisions, the Protection of Civil Rights Act of 1955 and the Prevention of Atrocities Act of 1989. The tribals are expected to be the main beneficiaries of welfare legislation of general applicability pertaining to land reforms, bonded labour, minimum wages and debt relief, etc. It appears that there are adequate legal armoury to safeguard the interests of the tribals in India. But in reality, atrocities against them have continued unabated.

The protective and development measures taken by the Government like allotment of surplus lands, release of bonded labour and implementation of minimum wages have antagonised the traditional land owning classes in the rural and tribal areas. This resentment has manifested itself, in many cases, in the shape of organised, collective violence against the tribals.

Recognising the vulnerable position of tribals, the constitution vested enormous powers for administration and control of tribal areas. However, such powers are never enforced.

Dispossession of tribal lands, a source of unrest and violence in tribal areas has not been systematically checked. On the other hand, cases have come to light of, patwaris colluding in the expropriation of tribals and settlement officials assisting in the regularisation of illegal transactions in tribal lands. Tightening up of administration in these areas is clearly called for along with exercise of powers under Schedule V whenever necessary.

It has been observed that the revenue oriented forest and excise policies of Government have disrupted the tribal economy and the tribal way of life. The emphasis on commercial exploitation of forests for industrial raw material has resulted in large scale displacement of tribals from their lands and homes. Tribal women have become even more vulnerable because of the exodus of men in search of employment. The operation of excise contractors in the tribal areas has led tribals into debt and eventual displacement.

There is clear need for Government to weigh revenue considerations against tribal welfare and strike the proper balance. Failing this, Government policies themselves will sow the seeds for atrocities against the tribals.

Against a backdrop where the grip of the land-lord and money-lender still persists in rural areas, where the lower bureaucracy ally themselves to the power groups, where atrocity cases against Tribes get low priority, a more dynamic role has necessarily to be played by State sponsored legal aid. Voluntary Organisations have paramount role to play in securing redress in atrocity cases.

It is seen that though land disputes, indebtedness, bonded labour, wages are proximate causes of atrocities, the root causes are poverty and illiteracy. The policy making levels of Government have realised that the benefits of developmental expenditure do not automatically trickle down to the weaker sections. Poverty alleviation schemes and special socio-economic programmes for the Scheduled Tribes are therefore, being implemented. The full impact will not be felt unless the administration of these programmes is decentralised and unless Scheduled Tribes are closely associated with fixing priorities, selecting beneficiaries and deciding on timing of assistance. The siphoning off of Government assistance, by development brokers, who prey mainly on SC/ST schemes should be eliminated. Schemes for Scheduled Castes and Tribes should lay special emphasis on creation of entrepreneurship.

In the light of the aforesaid discussion, it is highly imperative to have a fresh look at the tribal problems for visible socio-economic transformation and integration of tribals into the national mainstream.

"Tribal Development in India"—contains eleven contributions of eminent authors relating to various issues and problems of tribals along with policy options. The role of financial institutions, co-operatives in mitigating the tribal economic problems, the impact of developmental plans and poverty amelioration schemes, etc., have been discussed at length.

Based on secondary as well as field data this work portrays

the evaluation and analysis of tribal problems, policy paradigms to tackle the problem of backwardness in tribal regions.

The papers included in this volume mainly categorised into four sections Prof. Joshi's paper 'Acceleration of Tribals' deals with problem of Bhil tribe of Gujarat. The non-tribals and Bhils elites have enjoyed the lion's share in the distributive system of benefits under the processes of modernisation and constitutional safeguards. The Bhil tribals have become victims of indebtedness and exploitation. Ultimately, these problems culminate in the dispossession of lands, migration and mobilisation of labour. Prof. Joshi has observed that the Bhils are keenly interested to maintain their social identity.

In this context it is relevant to mention that the resultant effect of interactions between tribes and non-tribals may be conceived in terms of acculturation, assimilation, and integration. Acculturation has been understood as a process of subsequent change in the original cultural patterns of either tribes or both tribes and non-tribes. The process of assimilation has been viewed in terms of loss of identification and cultural identity on the part of numerically smaller tribes who became a part of non-tribe Indian civilization. Integration has been considered as a continuing process of mutual *quid-pro-quo* relation between tribes and non-tribes.

Dr. Das and Dr. Sahu in their paper, "A changing socio-demographic scenario of the Sauras in Orissa " have analysed the socio-economic and demographic scenario of Saura tribe through field study in Chandragiri locality of Ganjam district of Orissa. The sample households were studied through structured schedules which contained important variables like size of the family, sex-ratio, level of education, occupational status, level of income, marital status, problem of health and mortality, etc. The study endeavoured to point out the impact of influences of Hindu and Christian religions on various Saura Community and consequent changes taking place in the tribal life and socio-economy.

Dr. Mahapatra's paper on 'Socio-economic and cultural life of Kandhas of Orissa' portrays a vivid picture of agricultural production and system of cultivation adopted by Kandhas, their system of marriage, festivals and worship of various Gods and

Goddesses and finally on their socio-economic life.

Impact of Government Schemes and plan programmes on tribals of Orissa in general and Phulbani tribals in particular have been analysed in the papers of Mr. C.R. Dash and Dr. Tripathy, respectively.

Impact of financial institutions and co-operatives in the socio-economic life of tribals have been discussed in three papers of Dr. Eswar Rao Patnaik, Dr. Tripathy and Dr. Samantaray.

Dr. Patnaik's study is confined to a backward tribal district—Koraput (un-divided) of Orissa. The study highlights the performance of Commercial banks, Regional Rural Banks and Co-operatives and their impact in the socio-economic life of tribals of Koraput. Presenting a brief over-view of literature on tribal studies Dr. Patnaik through field studies on the basis of multi-stage random sampling technique has discussed the institutional and non-institutional sources of finance to the tribals for agriculture and other allied activities.

The study concluded with the observation that there has been an impressive increase in the relative share of institutional sources of finance for agriculture in Koraput (Orissa).

Assessing briefly the tribal demography and constitutional provisions, the problem of tribal marketing and the role of LAMPS in enhancing tribal economy of Phulbani has been presented in Dr. Tripathy"s paper, "Co-operatives for Tribal Development in Orissa."

Dr. Samantaray's paper "Role of Tribal Development Co-operative Corporation in Orissa" presenting an introductory note on tribal population, their socio-economic profile, tribal development strategy adopted during plan periods, evaluates the role of tribal development co-operative corporation (TDCC). The paper not only examines the activities of TDCC but also studies the associated problems with remedial suggestions for policy implications.

Empowerment of tribals and human resources development in tribal regions of Gujarat state through education and increasing the status of health of tribals in Rajasthan have been out-lined in two unique papers of Dr. Masavi and Dr. Nagda respectively.

Dr. Masavi in his paper, "Human Resources Development in tribal areas" has focused on the imperative needs of educational development in tribal regions of Gujarat. Further, the paper examines the literacy position of Gujarat tribals during various census operations. Factors responsible for high incidence of wastage and stagnation in Gujarat state, the extent of poverty and reasons of drop-outs have also been touched in this paper.

Dr. Nagda analyses the tribal scenario of Rajasthan state and the strategy of Sub-Plan adopted for the development of tribals. Through field survey method he exhibits various indicators of health components like level of mortality, incidence of mortality by age and sex, infant and child mortality, the state of sanitation and hygiene, child rearing practices and reproductive health.

Dr. Zathik Ali in his paper studied the problems and living conditions of Rubber plantation tribal workers of Kerala state. A vivid description of various aspects of labourers, their classification, hours of work, wage structure, labour welfare and social security schemes, various Acts, the position of women and child labourers, etc., have been made in this paper.

Indeed, the present volume could not have been brought to light without the contribution of papers by the eminent authors and researchers. The editor expresses his deepest gratitude to all the contributors whose papers have enriched this volume.

It is hoped that the book will be immensely useful in guiding the policy makers, planners, tribal administrators, researchers in formulating policy for tribal development in our country.

The hearty co-operation of may wife Meera Rani, son Sameer and daughter Sumita are memorable; in the completion of editing. The neglect inflicted on them during the course of this editing could be compensated if the general public will exhibit their sympathy towards the innumerable tribals and neglected aboriginals of our country.

Finally, I express my deep gratitude to Mr. T.R. Wasan, Discovery Publishing House for publishing the work within record time.

Dr. S.N. Tripathy

Dr. Masavi in his paper, 'Human Resources Development in Gujarat', has focused on the imperative needs of educational development in the society of Gujarat. Further, the paper examines the literacy position of [illegible] tribals [illegible] various operations, factors responsible for high incidence of wastage and stagnation in Gujarat state. The extent of poverty and aspects of [illegible] have also been touched in this paper.

[illegible] the state and the strategy [illegible] adoption of the development [illegible]. [illegible] with various indicators of health [illegible] the level of mortality, incidence of [illegible] mortality, the state of sanitation and hygiene, child rearing practices and reproductive health.

Dr. Zahik Ali in his paper studies the problems and living conditions of Rubber plantation [illegible] of Kerala state. A [illegible] description of various aspects [illegible] the [illegible] wage [illegible] and social security [illegible] and child labourers have been made [illegible] paper.

Indeed, the present volume could not have been brought without the [illegible] and [illegible] to all the contributors who have [illegible].

[illegible] the book will be [illegible] the policy makers, planners, academicians, researchers [illegible]

[illegible]

Contents

1

Acceleration of Tribals

Prof (Dr.) Sarat T. Joshi*

Where do the Tribals stand today is a question? Are they benefited by the government measures? Are they uprooted? Have they retained their social and cultural identity? Which areas have been accelerated? What is the structure of the *modus operandi* of the tribal development? Who takes enough benefit of the tribal area planning? How far the tribal development be differentiated from the general development of the country? What benefits are taken by the Non tribals? Whether tribals have been integrated in the mainstream keeping secular principals of indian Constitution?

The reply of the above questions have remained unanswered or say questions giving rise to questions more and more till the Indian arithmetic brings the result zero in spite of many steps in the equations. Step by step the movement is wrong, and the ultimate result is the defeat of poor Bhil. In this game of planners is beaten from all the sides, till he is mentally dead. It is nothing but the uprooting of these innocent active Bhils.

Where is acceleration? There is an introduction of the target

* *Prof. Joshi is a retired Professor of Sociology of Gujarat University. As an eminent sociologist he was awarded the UGC and ICSSR fellowship forcarrying out various research projects.*

group programmes to improve the quality of the life of the Tribal people. Processes of modernization of agriculture, constitutional safeguards giving advantages to scheduled tribes changed the subsistence economy to capitalist economy, local market work to world market. When we think of tribal transformation and tribal stratification the distributive system of benefits should be accounted for. The Non-tribals and the Bhils elites have taken the major advantages of the planning. The majority of the Bhils have failed to get their bare necessities of life. Not only that but this capital intensive planning of the government gave rise to various contradictions and complexities in the social structure of the Bhil tribals, yet they have maintained their social identity which had been the base of their demand for autonomous or separate statehood in the country say Bhilistan.

Today, the Poor Bhil is running here and there in search of employment to keep his body and soul together. The structure of the distribution system of benefits has led the scheduled sections to class contradictions yet it is observed that in the Post independent period, the compound growth rate for all crops during 22 years (1952-73) was substantially higher for Gujarat (4.44%) compared to all India 2. 51%.

There is necessity to integrate the tribal people in the national mainstream but the national mainstream is very wide. It can be fractioned in Economic mainstream, Political mainstream, Social mainstream, Cultural mainstream-(Education, etc.). Unfortunately, the main purpose to integrate these tribals with the advanced groups is left aside and there are innumerable problems that have emerged on account of their so called integration in the national mainstream. "Chaos of Values" and "Counter values" and the consequent break up of the social structure. The contacts of the tribals with the urban people have also created problems of adjustment. The Tribals suffer also due to inferiority complex. In their native places, also, there are problems of fractions of land. The fertility of land also gets reduced due to carelessness. There is heavy economic loss due to indiscriminate deforestation by the government. The Bhil tribals have become victims of indebtedness and exploitation and these emerges problems of the dispossession of lands, migration and mobilisation of labour. The national attributes of democracy, socialism and secularism seems yet to be achieved when there are contradictions and complexities emerging due to constitutional safeguards.

CHANGES AT MESO, MACRO AND MICRO

Each tribal group has its own historical individuality. The different tribes of India have its pecular characteristics but there is very little marginal differentiation between the Bhils of Panchmahals and the Bhils of other states. Whatever available observations are shown as under along with the traditional attributes. The Bhils prefer to maintain their social identity at any cost. Various studies show the similar attributes among the tribals yet the few attributes delineated by S.L. Joshi in his work "Tribal Ethnictiy class and Integration" are 1. Scattered Pattern of Habitation 2. Religion 3. Language 4. Life style 5. Institutions— polygamy, bride price, Women status, drinking, etc. 6. Subsistence Economy 7. Fairs and Festivals. Our observations during the field work referring the above attributes during post Independence Period are as under :

---

1. Scattered Pattern of Living: Bhils used to live in hills and forests and scattered villages. Houses are seen on hillocks. Hardly there may be one or two sanitary wells in a village, two or three houses in a scattered village may be close to a well but the rest at a distance of 5 km or more than that. Similarly, electrification or water supply through pipes may not be possible. At the same time Pattern of habitation is compact. Houses closer to cach other and fields at a distance The falias (neighbourhoods) are located at the fringe of the village.

1. Observations of this particular attribute of scattered pattern of habitation. There are a few changes in the agricultural methods. The youngsters prefer to use HYV insecticides, manure, etc., for better produce and at times use new inputs but his pattern of living has very minor change. The young affinal kjn prefers his own falia which may be a compact one. Similarly, he may use bricks in building houses but the agricultural construction is of the old type. He brings furniture and utensils of steel but the general patterns of the house and the village has the same traditionality. Bhils (Bhagat) in Kadwal (Jhalod Taluka) are having better economic condition, but their pattern of living is the same, traditional. Throughout the study of various villages in Panchmahals. Bhils may be iliterate, educated or rich or poor, prefers to live in his own traditional style.

2. Religion: The tribal form of religion was animism, tribal animism where magic is the pre-dominant element. Beliefs in spirits, ghosts, witchcrafts, etc.—omens good or bad.

2. Hinduism has some impact on Bhils. He at times worships Hindu Gods and goddesses. But at the same time, he has full faith in his village deity. He prays to this diety when in calamity or

	bad rains or crisis, etc. The married couple pay respect to ancestral Gods. Here, a little change due to Hindu impact but yet the village traditions of religion are not left out. The rituals are the same. Belief in transmigration of soul continues. Heaven and Hell ideology continues.
3. Language: The Bhils used to speak in Bhilli language but later on some ınixture was witnessed.	3. In groups of their own they prefer to speak in their traditional dialect. But Vagadi and Hindu dialect is mixed with the Bhilli dialect. A little change is seen in Gujarat region in dialect, maybe a mixture of Gujarati, Hindi, Bhilli and Vagadi too.
4. Institutions: Marriage—Woman is a property as obtained by paying bride price. Sex-laxity is seen. Polygamy existed. Notra gift presentation in cash and corn.	4. Marriage—Monogamy highly practised. Polygamy getting reduced day by day, may be due to economic situation of a Bhil also. But the system of Notra still continues. Bride price is getting reduced gradually. (Depends on Education) Death: Death feasts not visible.
5. Drinking liquor, etc. Liquor found on all occasions, child birth, marriage, death, Holi and Diwali festivals.	5. In spite of legal prohibition, drinking is still continued. It has become a strong custom also. Wine and Women are still prevaiting attributes to a large extent. Most of the quarrels are also due to Land, Lady and Liquor. This evil has become practically custom on all occasions.

Various other studies have also been made delineating other areas of the tribal life in our village level. Taluka level and District level, a few observations were made while studying a few areas. (Micro level, Macro level and Meso level.)

Village (Micro level)	*Taluka (Macro Level)*	*District (Meso Level)*
Diet:		
The same Traditional diet	A little change due to urban contacts, good food.	A little more change, good food with Achars (Pickles) be the quality and vegetables.
Clothes:		
Dhoti, cap and old shirt, bare-footed, women, cloth round the waste, very few clothes. A Bhil woman is seen with log of wood for fire on head also to sell in towns.	Dhoti, Trousers, Shirt. Cap is removed at times. Shoes or chapals, women sari and full clothes, urban effect.	Trousers, Pants, Shirt, Dhoti shoes or chapals better quality dress. Urban impact.
Vehicles:		
Mostly moving on foot, Bullock cart or some animal to go a long distance, at times cycle.	Cycle, animals, Two wheeler, at times for affluent Bhils. Bullock cart also used.	Two or at times four wheeler, cycle, bullock cart, etc. Modernization in using vehicles observed.
Utensils:		
For cooking clay, aluminium, Brass same old methods wood, etc. At times gober gas (sometimes) but very few cases.	Steel, Hindalium, Brass a little change can be seen in cooking at times cooking gas also used.	Cooking gas and vessels of steel, Brass, Hindalium. A good change in life style.
Furniture old type.	Furniture Modernized—Radio, Changer, T.V.	Modernized furniture, chairs, sofas, tepoys, Radio, Musical Circuits. T.V., Modern instruments of good manufacture.
Crops		
Maize, Jowar, Tuer.	Cash Crops—Cotton, Rice introduced.	Cash crops—Cotton Rice, commercialisation of crops.
Marriage, Death, etc.		
Bridegroom either on foot or some vehicle. Long coat, kalgi (Hair Pin) old style of clothes in marriage. Liquor enough. Food from vegetables ghee, oil—lapsi (Sweet from wheat) Rice (Mostly sweet) Vegetables, Puri (bread)	No death feasts. Notra ritual observed in marriages. Food from oil, vegetable ghee. Ready sweets of better quality from shops. Namkin, Tuer Dal, Vegetables, etc., Chapati, puri, pickles, etc., good food sitting in chairs.	No death feasts. Good food at marriages of affording people, good sweets with vegetables. Tuer Dal and a few varieties, sitting in chairs, music also better, adorning of houses. Band musics.
Death feasts prohibited now. Bride price and	Music at marriage, good adorning of houses.	Bridegroom in cars. Silver and

child marriages a little change. Notra ritual observed. Sitting on floor only. Plastic bangles and at times silver in marriage.	Band musics. Bridegroom in vehicles. Silver and gold ornaments	gold, precious ornaments.
No ploygamy.	No polygamy.	No polygamy.
Bondage still continues—very little cash income.	No bondage seen, labourers daily wages. Good cash income.	No bondage seen. Labourers daily or monthly wages, better cash income.
No medical facilities.	Somewhat medical facilities in hospitals by Govt. or health centres.	Good medical facilities, good hospitals also.
Education: Hardly Primary education	Secondary, Higher Secondary and College Education.	Secondary, Higher Secondary College up to Post Graduation.
No Electricity in most of villages. No diesel Engine or Irrigation wells.	Wells, Irrigation, somewhat use of diesel engines. Electrification good.	Irrigation facilities better, diesel engines, pumps, etc., used.
Exploitation, bondage, etc. Heavy interest of Shahukars.	Exploitation is observed. Low payments.	Exploitation is seen
Native Bhils, Bhagat Bhils, Bhilli dialect.	Bhagat Bhils and Christian Bhils. Bhilli mixed with Hindi and Gujarati, Vagadi dialect.	Bhagat Bhils and Christian Bhils, Bhilli, Hindi, Gujarati, Vagadi, etc.
Wood cutting traditional agriculture.	Stone-cutting, labourers, Ramalas (household servants) salaried government servants.	Stone cutting, Ramalas (house-hold servants, Dally wages on roads, buildings, gangmen salaried government servants.
Labour mostly as Capital.	Labour mostly as capital except a few affluents.	Labour mostly as Capital except affluent class.
No elitism—subsistence economy.	Elitism, market economy, Political elites, Panchayat leaders. Government servants.	Elitism, world market economy entrepreneurs, etc. Government servants Poltical leaders.

2

A Changing Socio-Demographic Scenario of the Sauras in Orissa

Dr. N.C. Das[1]
Dr. S.K. Sahu[2]

Sauras are one of the major tribes of Orissa. They are known by different names such as Saora, Sora, Savara, Sabara and Saar. However, all of them belong to one tribe, showing their racial affinity with the Proto-Australoids. The Saura languages comes under the Mundari group of Austric family. However, due to constant interaction with the neighbouring Oriya people they have accepted Oriya as their second language. Sauras are mainaly distributed in Ganjam, Gajapati and Koraput Districts of Orissa. They are also found in the adjacent districts of Andhra Pradesh. There are three broad divisions of the tribe such as the Lanjia (Primitive). the Sudha (Hinduised) and the Christian (converted) Sauras. The latter two groups are the accultured (changed) categories, whereas the Lanjias are the primitive and the original Sauras.

The common identity of Lanjia Saura is expressed in their religious beliefs and rituals such as worship of common spirits and ghosts. This group mostly depends on shifting cultivation along with

1. *Reader in Anthropology, Khallikote (Auto) College, Berhampur, Orissa.*
2. *Lecturer in Economics, K.S.U.B. College, Bhanjanagar, Orissa.*

hunting and food gathering as their livelihood. Economically, they are most backward compared to the other two groups.

The Sudha Saura exhibits many cultural features of the Hindus. They have accepted plane cultivation being influenced by the neighbouring Hindus. As a result the Sudha Saura villages are mostly found in the foothills. Besides, they also practice animal husbandry and various indigenous economic pursuits.

The Christian Sauras who have accepted Christianity belong to Primitive (Lanjia) section of the community. The adaption of a new religion has separated them from the other two sections of the Saura. However, the Christian Sauras still observe the lineage (Birinda) exogamy as that of the Lanjia Saura. Economically, the Christian Sauras are better off compared to their counterparts, as they get donations, both in cash and kind, from the missionaries along with health and educational benefits. Further, in spite of their conversion to Christianity they also avail the government concessions and other facilities similar to the primitive Sauras.

The present paper highlights the socio-economic and demographic scenario of the above three categories of the Sauras in a comparative way.

METHODS OF STUDY

The present paper is based on the original empirical work, covering 26 villages in total. Data were collected from 218 Lanjia households, 212 Sudha households and 227 Christian households. Three different types of structured schedules such as (I) Household census schedule (II) Schedule for marriage and fertility (III) Schedule for disease and mortality. The above schedules were canvased among the various households for getting necessary data. For filling in the schedules interview technique was adopted. Further, observation method, particularly non-participant type was also adhered to for recording various informations. The enumeration was conducted on door to door contact basis. The help of village head men, village school teachers, village level workers, Sarpanches, and Priests of Churches and other village elites were also sought for.

FINDINGS

The findings of the study have been analysed under the following broad categories.

FAMILY SIZE

Family is the smallest social unit. It is observed that only the consanguneal kins constitute the households. Joint families are commonly noticed among the Sudha Sauras. This shows that the Sudhas have accepted the Hindu way of joint family system. Such joint family system is not found either among the primitive tribes or among the christians. However, Table 2.1 shows that the Lanjias have a higher family size. This contrasting findings is justified because Lanjia fertility is higher (discussed latter) and they also receive all types of help from the Saura Development Agency (S.D.A.)

TABLE 2.1 DISTRIBUTION OF FAMILY SIZE

Household :	1	2	3	4	5	6	7	8	9	*Total*
Lanjia :	0	9	42	48	56	29	16	13	5	218
	0	(4.12)	(19.26)	(22.0)	(25.68)	(13.30)	(7.33)	(5.96)	(2.29)	(100)
Sudha :	3	22	28	34	52	49	17	7	5	212
	(1.41	(10.37)	(13.20)	(16.03)	(24.52)	(22.11)	(8.01)	(3.30)	(2.5)	(100)
Christ. :	1	11	56	57	46	34	14	5	3	227
	(0.44)	(4.85)	(24.69)	(25.11)	(20.26)	(14.98)	(6.19)	(2.20)	(1.32)	(100)

(Average family size : Lanjia - 4.82, Sudha - 4.77, Christian - 4.48)

Table 2.1 reveals that the Christian Sauras have comparatively a smaller family size. This changed scenario is possible due to the constant influence of the Christian Missionaries.

POPULATION STRUCTURE AND COMPOSITION

The population structure and composition of the selected Saura villages show an interesting feature. The 218 Lanjia, 212 Sudha and 227 Christian households have a population of 1051, 1011 and 1018 individuals respectively. It is found that proportion of female population in case of Lanjia Saura is more than the males but in case of Sudha and Christian Saura the proportion of male is comparatively high.

TABLE 2.2: DISTRIBUTION OF SAURA POPULATION

Section of Saura	*Male*	*(%)*	*Female*	*(%)*	*Total*	*(%)*	*Sex Ratio (M/Fx1000)*
Lanjia	523	(49.78)	528	(50.24)	1051	(100)	990
Sudha	544	(53.81)	469	(46.19)	1011	(100)	1165
Christian	519	(50.98)	499	(49.02)	1018	(100)	1040

It is noticed that the sex ratio of Lanjia is 990 males per 1000 females. This is a case of low sex ratio which favours the females. In case of Sudha Sauras, the sex ratio is 1165 males for 1000 females. This is a case of high sex ratio which favours the males. However, the sex ratio of the Christian Saura is in between Lanjia and Sudha that is 1040 males per 1000 females which also favours the males. It is observed that the status of women among Lanjia Saura is more or less balanced. But the women in case of Sudha and Christian Saura enjoy somewhat low status (this requires further investigation). Further, it is also noticed (discussed under mortality) that the male death rates among the Lanjia and female death rates among the Sudha and the Christian are relatively high. Of course, migration factor was not considered while discussing the sex ratio. However, we are sure that the impact of migration on sex ratio must be negligible.

EDUCATIONAL STANDARD

The socio-economic status of a community depends on the educational standard of the people. Educational standard is also an indicator of economic development. The following data in Table 2.3 reveals a changing scenario of the educational standard of the three sections of the Sauras.

TABLE 2.3 PERCENTAGE DISTRIBUTION OF EDUCATIONAL STANDARD

Sections of Saura	Illi-terate	Below L. P.	Up to L. P.	Up to U.P.	Up to M.E.	Up to H.Sc	Beyond H.Sc.	Total Literate
Lanjia	78.42	12.83	4.00	1.66	1.77	1.22	0.12	1.57
Sudha	58.7	20.00	5.50	6.40	3.10	5.40	0.80	41.30
Christ.	77.50	19.58	0.82	0.82	0.58	0.70	-	22.50

(Children below 5 years are excluded)

The study shows that the total literates among Lanjia, Sudha and Christian are 21.6%, 41.3% and 22.5% respectively. The percentage of literates among Lanjias and Christians are far behind compared to the state literacy figures, i.e., 49% as per 1991 census. But the Sudhas are not lagging far behind compared to state figure. The total illiterate among Lanjia, Sudha and Christian are 78.4%, 58.7% and 77.5% respectively.

From the above analysis it is clear that the Sudhas are more advanced in literacy compared to other two sections of the tribe. Table 2.3 depicts the educational standard from L.P. to beyond Matriculation of Lanjia is better than Christian Sauras. But as per the total literacy is concerned the Christians show a higher percentage (22.5) than the Lanjias (21.5). It is because in below lower primary level the Christian children are much ahead than the Lanjia children. This may be due to the immediate effect of the Christian missionaries. In spite of the motivation and various helps from the missionaries these people are lagging far behind in education in comparison to the state standard. The Lanjias are also lagging behind in total literacy but without any motivation or assistance. However, the Sudhas are much ahead in education among all the three Saura categories. This might be due to impact of the Hindu way of life, culture and philosophy.

The tribal education is of great importance for economic development of the state as a whole. So, the government is taking much interest in tribal education, at present. Hence, concerted effort is highly essential to bring the Saura educational standard at par with the state standard.

OCCUPATIONAL STATUS

It is observed that majority of the tribals in all the three sections are engaged in cultivation. The plane and terrace cultivation are commonly found among the three sections of the Sauras. It is further observed that there is a meagre difference between primary and secondary occupation. It is noticed that 60.30% of the population among the three sections of the Sauras are workers, Table 2.4.

TABLE 2.4: DISTRIBUTION OF SAURA WORKERS BY BROAD AGE GROUP

Sections of Saura	*Child age group (below-15)*	*Eco-active age group (15-59)*	*Aged Group (60 & above) (in per cent)*	*Total workers*
Lanjia	3.85	96.00	44.00	61.00
Sudha	15.70	76.30	36.11	55.10
Christian	23.40	97.50	50.00	64.74

It is noticed that from the economic active age group (15.59), as large as 96% among the Lanjias, 76% among the Sudhas and 97% among the Christian are engaged in various economic activities. In view of the above workers population, we can say the Saura is an active tribe. Of course, they don't get an opportunity to work throughout the year. Further, more than 13% among Lanjias, 15% among Sudhas and 23% among Christian Sauras in the child population are active workers. Comparatively, maximum Christian children are active workers. This change might be due to the impact of Christian missionaries. Among the aged males 44% Lanjias, 39% Sudhas and 50% Christians are actively engaged in various economic activities.

It is also observed that the Sauras are engaged in government service which is a remarkable feature. This indicates that at present the Sauras are gradually accepting secondary and tertiary jobs.

The total workers are more than 60% among Lanjia, 55% among Sudha and more than 64% among the Christian Saura of the total population of respective sections.

It is also found that very less Saura population have accepted business as an occupation. They also collect and sell forest produce in the nearby market. It is interesting to note that the Christian Sauras do not undertake business as an occupation.

INCOME AND EXPENDITURE

The entire income and expenditure of the family from different sources have been calculated and categorised by monthly basis.

Income determines the standard of living of the family whereas the expenditure recognises the consumption pattern of the family.

TABLE 2.5: DISTRIBUTION OF AVERAGE MONTHLY INCOME AND EXPENDITURE OF SAURAS

Sections of Saura	*Average monthly Income*	*Annual per capita Income*	*Average monthly Expenditure*	*Average per capita Expenditure*
Lanjia	514	1284	526	1309
Sudha	641	1608	650	1635
Christian	492	1320	521	1395

Table 2.5 reveals the average income and average expenditure of the three sections of the Saura. Both the average income and expenditure have been calculated taking seven income and expenditure slabs. Similarly, nine different family categories have been taken for analysis, the lowest being one member family and the highest is 9 members and above.

The Sudhas show the highest family income, average being Rs. 641/-, the Christians show the lowest income with an average of Rs. 492/- per month, and the Lanjias enjoy the middle status as their average income is Rs. 541/- per month. From the above analysis it is clear that the Lanjias and Christians more or less belong to one economic class whereas the Sudhas are at a higher income level. The per capita income of Lanjia, Sudha and Christian Sauras are Rs. 1284/-, Rs. 1608/- and Rs. 1320/- respectively. The per capita income of Christians are more than the Lanjias (though the average income of Lanjias is high) is due to the lower family size of Christians (4.48).

The average expenditure of the Lanjia, the Sudha, and the Christian Sauras are Rs. 526/-, Rs. 650/- and Rs. 521/- respectively. Table 2.5 clearly shows that all the three sections of the tribe spend more than their income. However, the Christian Sauras on an average spend more than their income compared to the other two sections of the tribe. This is because they are being helped both in cash and kind by the Christian missionaries. The expenditure schedule determines the consumption pattern of the individuals. The Christian Sauras, being converted, possess a changed way of life which determines their consumption pattern. The change in way of life multiplies their wants and hence the consumption pattern. Thus the expenditure of the Christian Sauras has increased under changed circumstances.

The Lanjias are being helped by Saura Development (SDA) located at Chandragiri so they are able to spend more. But the Sudhas neither get any help from government sector nor from non-government organisations (N.G.O.). They borrow from their class friends and local money lenders to meet their expenses.

MARITIAL STATUS

Maritial status in any demographic study provides the fundamental information regarding the vulnerable group responsible for fertility. The data in Table 2.6 clearly states the differential maritial status of the three sections of the Saura.

TABE 2.6 DISTRIBUTION OF SAURA POPULATION BY MARITIAL STATUS

Sections of Saura	*Unmarried* *M*	*F*	*Married* *M*	*F*	*Widowed* *M*	*F*	*Div/Sep* *M*	*F*	*EverMarried* *M*	*F*	*Total* *M*	*F*
Lanjia	296	276	201	205*	22	34	4	13	227	252	523	528
	(56.6)	(52.3)	(38.4)	(38.8)	(4.2)	(6.4)	(0.8)	(2.5)	(43.4)	(47.7)	(100)	(100)
Sudha	299	205	231	231	12	24	2	7	245	262	544	467
	(55.0)	(43.9)	(42.4)	(50.0)	(2.2)	(5.1)	(0.3)	(1.5)	(45.0)	(56.1)	(100)	(100)
Christ.	290	255	214	214	10	16	5	14	229	244	519	499
	(55.9)	(51.1)	(40.1)	(43.5)	(1.9)	(3.2)	(0.9)	(2.8)	(43.3)	(48.6)	(100)	(100)

(* Lanjia male accepted two wives: cases of polygyny)

It is evident from Table 2.6 that the percentage of unmarried males among the Lanjia, the Sudha and the Christian are 57%; 55%, 56% and females are 52%, 44%, 51% respectively. It is found from Table 2.6 that a large number of males and females are unmarried among the Lanjia Saura than that of the other two sections. However, a low percentage of Sudha women are unmarried in comparision to their counterparts. This change could possibly be due to the influence of their Hindu neighbours. It is also observed that the percentage of currently married males among the Lanjia, the Sudha and the Christian Sauras are 38%, 42%, 41% and currently married females are 38%, 49% and 43% respectively. It is found that comparatively a large number of Sudha males and females are currently married among the three sections of the tribe.

The widowed, divorced and separated females among the Lanjia, the Sudha and the Christian are 9%, 7% and 5% and the corresponding male figures are 5%, 2.5% and 2.6% respectively. From this it is clear that large number of widowed, divorced and separated males remarried compared to females. The practice of polygyny among the Lanjia Sauras was observed during the time of data collection. The data in Table 2.6 show the imbalance between the currently married males and females (male-201, female-205) among the Lanjia Saura is due to the presence of four polygamous families. The polygamous families are not observed among the Sudha and the Christian Sauras during data collection. This change towards monogamy is due to the influence of Hindu and Christian religions.

AGE AT MARRIAGE

Age at marriage is an important social as well as demographic factor which influences the child bearing period and also determines the fertility of the community. The average age of first marriage of the Lanjia, the Sudha and the Christian males are 22.7, 22.6 and 23.2 years and of females 18.4, 18.6 and 20.4 years respectively, Table 2.7.

TABLE-2.7 DISTRIBUTION OF EVER MARRIED SAURA POPULATION BY AGE AT FIRST MARRIAGE

	Age at first marriage											
Sections of Saura	*below-15*		*15-19*		*20-24*		*25-29*		*30 above*		*Total*	
	M	*F*	*M*	*F*	*M*	*F*	*M*	*F*	*M*	*F*	*M*	*F*
Lanjia	1	18	33	148	150	85	41	1	2	-	227	252
	(0.4)	(7.1)	(914.1)	(58.7)	(66.1)	(33.7)	(18.1)	(0.4)	(0.9)	(-)	(100)	(100)
Sudha	2	24	46	152	123	84	71	2	3	-	245	262
	(0.8)	(9.1)	(18.7)	(58.0)	(50.2)	(32.1)	(28.4)	(0.7)	(1.2)	(-)	(100)	(100)
Christ.			33	114	131	118	65	12	-	-	229	244
	(-)	(-)	(14.5)	(46.4)	(57.2)	(48.3)	(28.4)	(4.8)	(-)	(-)	(100)	(100)

(Average age of first marriage Lanjia - male 22.7 and female 18.4, Sudha - male 22.6 and female 18.6 and Christian male 23.2 and female 20.4)

Table 2.7 indicates that maximum number of Lanjia and Sudha females marry inbetween 15 to 19 years of age, 58.7% and 58% respectively. Further, maximum number of Lanjia and Sudha males marry inbetween 20 to 24 years of age, 66.1% and 50.2% respectively. However, in case of Christian Sauras maximum number of marriages for both male and female (48%) take place between 20 to 24 years of age. A very low percentage of marriages below 15 years of age are noticed among the females of Lanjia and Sudha. Interestingly, in case of Christian Sauras, marriages below 15 years of age are not found. This changing scenario of age at marriage is due to the impact of the Christian religion on this tribal society.

The average age of first marriage among Lanjia, Sudha and Christian Sauras are 22.7 years, 22.6 years and 23.2 years for males respectively, and 18.5 years, 18.6 years and 20.4 years for females respectively. It is interesting to note that the age of first marriage both for male and female of all the three sections of the community are above the Government recommended ages of marriage. This higher age of marriage is due to the cultural practices of both Lanjia and Sudhas. The influence of Christianity has contributed greatly for the high age of marriage among the Christian Sauras.

AGE OF WOMEN AT FIRST CHILD BIRTH

Age of women at first child birth reflects the actual age at which female enter into motherhood or the eventual entry of female into the actual fertility performance. Table 2.8 shows the distribution of ever married Saura women by their actual gap between the age at marriage and the first child birth.

TABLE 2.8 DISTRIBUTION OF EVER MARRIED SAURA WOMEN BY GAP BETWEEN AGE AT MARRIAGE AND FIRST CHILD BIRTH

	Gap between age at marriage and first child birth							
Sections of Saura	*Below 1 yr.*	*1-2*	*2-3*	*3-4*	*4-5*	*5 Yrs.*	*No Res.*	*Total ever married women*
Lanjia	44 (17.46)	77 (30.56)	49 (19.49)	26 (10.32)	18 (7.14)	14 (5.56)	24 (9.52)	252 (100)
Sudha	21 (8.0)	87 (33.20)	70 (26.71)	29 (11.06)	14 (5.34)	15 (5.72)	26 (9.92)	262 (100)
Christian	7 (2.87)	77 (31.56)	71 (29.00)	36 (14.75)	16 (6.56)	19 (7.79)	18 (7.38)	244 (100)

(Average gap: Lanjia 2.23yrs, Sudha 2.39yrs and Christian 2.65 yrs. No response women are excluded from the average calculation.)

The data in Table 2.8 reveal that the average gap between the age of marriage and the age at first child birth among the Lanjia is 2.23 years and those of Sudha and Christian are 2.39 years and 2.65 years respectively. This shows that the Christian Saura has a larger gap between the age at marriage and first child birth.

Further, Table 2.8 reveals that the largest distribution among the Lanjia, the Sudha and the Christian Saura is (30.56%, 33.20% and 31.56% respectively) found inbetween 1 to 2 years of gap. The lowest Lanjia respondents (5.56%) experienced their first child birth after a gap of 5 years from marriage. The lowest Sudha couples (5.3%) experienced their first child birth in between 4 to 5 years of gap from marriage but the lowest Christian couples (2.8%) experienced their first child birth within the first year of marriage.

It is also noticed that a few ever married couples among three sections of the tribe are childless at the time of interview, these are grouped under no response column. The percentage distribution of these childless couples among the Lanjia, the Sudha and the Christians are 9.5%, 9.8% and 7.4% respectively.

OPEN BIRTH INTERVAL

The time gap between the present age and the age of last child birth is known as the open birth interval. This is also another indicator of the actual reproductive span of the females. Open birth interval also speaks about the use of family planning method among the Saura couples.

TABLE 2.9 DISTRIBUTION OF SAURA EVER MARRIED WOMEN BY THE OPEN BIRTH INTERVAL

	Open birth interval.						
Sections of Saura	*0-3*	*4-7*	*8-11*	*12-15*	*15+*	*No. Res.*	*Total ever married women*
Lanjia	105 (41.67)	47 (18.65)	29 (11.51)	29 (11.51)	8 (3.17)	24 (9.52)	252 (100)
Sudha	103 (39.31)	54 (20.41)	19 (7.25)	34 (12.96)	26 (9.92)	26 (9.92)	262 (100)
Christian	92 (37.71)	68 (27.67)	26 (10.66)	21 (8.61)	19 (7.79)	18 (7.38)	244 (100)

(The average open birth interval among Lanjia, Sudha and Christian Saura are 5.33, 6.44 and 6.00 respectively. No response women are excluded from the average calculation).

The present study shows that the percentage distribution of women among the Lanjia, the Sudha and the Christian Sauras, who had their open birth interval within 3 years, are nearly 42%, 39% and 38% respectively. As large as 18.65% of Lanjia women have enjoyed the open birth interval in between 4 to 7 years, 11.51% each within 8 to 11 years and 12 to 15 years. A total of 20.61% Sudha women have enjoyed an interval of 4 to 7 years, about 7% within 8 to 11 years and 13% in between 12 to 15 years while as large as 27.87% Christian women have experienced an interval of open birth within 4 to 7 years, 10.66% in between 8 to 11 years and 8.61% within 12 to 15 years. The percentage distribution of women among the Lanjia, the Sudha and the Christian Sauras who had an open birth interval of 15 years and above are 3.17%, 9.92% and 7.79% respectively.

The average open birth interval among the Lanjia, the Sudha and the Christian are calculated to be 5.33 years, 6.44 years and 6 years respectively. This indicates the use of family planning methods either for spacing or for stopping child birth. Both Sudha and Christian Sauras show slightly greater open birth intervals than that of their Lanjia counterparts. This change is surely due to the impact of Hindu and Christian religion, education and exposure to various modern media.

AGE AT LAST CHILD BIRTH

Age at last child birth shows the actual completion of child bearing activities. In the present study the women who have completed their fecund period (45 years and above) are considered for the calculations of the age as last child birth. Table 2.10 gives a clear picture of the distribution of women above 45 years by their age at last child birth and children ever born.

Interestingly Table 2.10 shows that maximum women, among the Lanjia (32.2%) and Christian (30.18%) Sauras have their last child birth during 35-39 years of age. However, the maximum Sudha women (39.65%) experienced their last child birth during 30 to 34 years of age. As large as 13.56% Lanjia women experienced their last child birth during 40 to 44 years. 18.64% in between 30-34 years and about 27% before 30 years of age. Nearly 28% Sudha women during 35 to 39 years, 10.34% women in between 40 to 44 years and about 14% women before 30 years of age experienced their last child birth. As large as 24.53% Christian women during 40 to 44 years and 26.30% women had their last child birth in between 30 to 34 years of age and about 11% women experienced their last child birth before 30 years of age. However, the average age at last child birth among the Lanjia, the Sudha and the Christian Sauras are 34.26 years 34.23 years and 35.70 years respectively and average children born to them during these periods are 5.0, 5.1 and 4.8 respectively.

TABLE 2.10: DISTRIBUTION OF AGE AT LAST CHILD BIRTH OF THE SAURA WOMEN 45 YEARS AND ABOVE BY CHILDREN EVER BORN.

Sections of Saura	Age at last child birth							
	15-19	*20-24*	*25-29*	*30-34*	*35-39*	*40-44*	*No Res.*	*Total ever married women*
Lanjia	-	-	16	11	19	8	5	59
	(-)	(-)	(27.12)	(18.64)	(32.20)	(13.56)	(8.47)	(100)
Sudha	-	1	7	23	16	6	6	58
	(-)	(1.72)	(12.06)	(39.65)	(17.58)	(10.34)	(10.34)	(100)
Christian	1	2	3	15	16	13	3	53
	(1.89)	(3.97)	(5.66)	(26.30)	(30.18)	(24.53)	(5.66)	(100)

(The average age at last child birth among Lanjia, Sudha and Christians are 39.26, 34.23 and 35.70 years respectively, and also average children born are 4.98, 5.10 and 4.78 respectively. No response women are excluded from the average calculations).

It is found from Table 2.10 that the Sudha women usually begin their fertility schedule around 20 years. Hence, the affective child bearing period is only 16 years, almost a reduction of 14 years (average fecund period is 30 years). This reduction is possible because of several factors such as late age at marriage, widowhood, acceptance of fertility controlling measures and possibly due to under nutrition. Under nutrition is also important for reducing the fecund period, Das (1979). Agrawala (1973) has stated that on an average 10 to 13 years of effective fertile period is lost due to various factors and mostly because of wodowhood.

CHILDREN EVER BORN

The number of children ever born mainly depends on the duration of marriage. The duration of marriage is also an important indicator for knowing the actual period of fertility performance. Panda (1989) observed that Fecundity among tribal women is generally lower compared to the nontribal women. The average number of children born to the tribals is 2.5 whereas among the nontribal is 2.9. The number of children ever born and duration of marriage is shown in Table 2.11.

TABLE 2.11 DISTRIBUTION OF SAURA CHILDREN EVER BORN BY DURATION OF MARRIAGE.

	Children ever born										
Sections of Saura	*1*	*2*	*3*	*4*	*5*	*6*	*7*	*8*	*9*	*No. Res.*	*Total ever Married Women*
Lanjia	42 (16.67)	56 (22.22)	48 (19.04)	42 (16.67)	15 (5.95)	14 (5.55)	5 (1.98)	4 (1.58)	2 (0.79)	24 (9.52)	252 (100)
Sudha	39 (14.89)	37 (14.12)	45 (17.18)	38 (14.50)	30 (11.45)	29 (11.06)	8 (3.08)	6 (2.29)	4 (1.52)	26 (9.92)	262 (100)
Christ.	40 (16.39)	64 (26.23)	52 (21.31)	34 (13.93)	16 (6.56)	11 (4.51)	6 (2.46)	2 (0.82)	1 (0.41)	18 (7.38)	244 (100)

(The average duration of marriage and average children everborn during the period among Lanjia, Sudha and Christian are 13.7 yrs., 16.7 years, 16.4 years and 2.82, 3.3, and 2.9 respectively).

It is observed that during the average duration of marriage, the average number of children born to the Lanjia, Sudha and the Christian women are 2.8, 3.3 and 2.9 respectively. However, the maximum Lanjia women (22.22%) and Christian women (26.25%) have given birth to 2 children. The maximum number of Sudha women (17.18%) have given birth to 3 children. As long as 19.04% Lanjia and 21.3% Christian women gave birth to 3 children. Nearly 17% Lanjia, 15% Sudha and 14% Christian women gave birth to 4 children. The percentage distribution of women among the Lanjia, the Sudha and the Christian Sauras who gave birth to 5 and above children are 15.87%, 29.39% and 14.75% respectively. The above data show that the Sudha women have an edge ever the other two sections as regards children everborn.

CURRENT FERTILITY

Children born last year gives a clear picture of the current fertility. Further, from this data a good number of fertility measures can be obtained. Table 2.12 shows the children born last year (one year before the study) along with the age specific fertility of the three sections of the tribe.

TABLE 2.12 AGE SPECIFIC FERTILITY OF THE SAURA.

Sections of Saura	*No. of Women*	*No. of currently married women*	*Children born last year M.*	*F.*	*Total*	*A.S.F.R.*	*A.S.M.F.R*
Lanjia	250	180	25	23	48	1.014	1.559
Sudha	255	189	21	20	41	0.915	1.236
Christ.	236	173	21	18	39	0.942	1.197

From Table 2.12 the following fertility measurements are calculated and the necessary analysis has been made.

The crude birth rate (C.B.R. of the Lanjia, the Sudha, and the Christian Sauras are 48, 41 and 36 births per 1000 population respectively. The C.B.R. of Lanjia is the highest among the three sections of the tribe. Low literacy and high infant mortality are the chief causes of such a high birth rate.

The General Fertility Rate (G.F.R.) is the ratio of live births to the total fecund women. The G.F.R. and G.M.F.R. of the Lanjias, the Sudha and the Christian are 192 and 267, 161 and 217 and 166 and 225 respectively. The G.F.R. and G.M.F.R. of the Lanjias are the highest among the three sections of the tribe.

The total fertility rate (T.F.R.) and the total marital fertility rate (T.M.F.R.) among the Lanjias are 5.1 and 7.8 and among the Sudha are 4.6 and 6.2. However, among the Christians, they are 4.7 and 6.0 respectively. The T.F.R. and T.M.F.R. of the Lanjia is the highest among the three sections of the tribe.

The gross reproduction rate (G.R.R.) of the Lanjia, the Sudha and the Christians are calculated to be 2.43, 2.23 and 2.17 respectively. This shows that the Lanjia women are highly fertile.

The above measurements of fertility reveal that the Lanjia Saura has a high fertility schedule compared to the Sudha and the Christians. In other words the Sudha and the Christians possess low fertility compared to the Lanjia. This changing senario is possible due to the impact of Hindu and Christian religions.

FAMILY PLANNING PRACTICES

Family planning does not mean merely birth control rather it means the real welfare of the family. However, for the Sauras, it is confined to birth control only. Knowledge of family planning is very common among the three sections of the Saura tribe. However, these have a poor knowledge about their family welfare. The family planning methods currently used by the three sections of the tribe are as follows. They follow four methods such as (i) Sterilization (ii) Intro-Uterina Contraceptive Device (I.U.C.D.) (iii) Regular use of oral pills, (iv) Conventional centraceptive (CC). However, the Sauras are aware of some traditional methods since long in addition to the above stated modern methods. Table 2.13 shows the family planning methods which are in practice among the three sections of the tribe.

TABLE 2.13: DISTRIBUTION OF RESPONDENTS BY THE METHODS OF FAMILY PLANNING ACCEPTORS.

Total Respondents	C.C.	I.U.C.D.	Terminal method	Traditional method	Total	Total currently married Fecund women
Lanjia	5 (2.78)	9 (5.00)	45 (25.00)	7 (3.69)	66 (36.67)	180 (100)
Sudha	3 (1.58)	12 (6.35)	34 (17.99)	2 (1.06)	51 (26.98)	189 (100)
Christ.	- (-)	18 (10.40)	43 (24.86)	- (-)	61 (35.76)	173 (100)
Total (%)	8 (1.47)	39 (7.19)	122 (22.51)	9 (1.66)	178 (32.84)	542 (100)

Table 2.13 shows that the total acceptors among the Lanjia, the Sudha and the Christian are about 36%, 26% and 35% respectively. The total acceptors of the state is about 36% among the currently married fecund women, National Family Health Survey (1994). The sterilized persons among the three sections of the tribe are in majority, i.e., about 22 per cent. The next higher proportion (7.19%) of acceptors have preferred Intra-Uterine Contraceptive Device (I.U.C.D). The Lanjias and the Sudhas preferred traditional method (1.66%) than the conventional contraceptives (1.47%). But the Christian Saura neither appreciate conventional contraceptives

nor the traditional methods. The couple protection rate among the Lanjia, the Sudha and the Christians are 31.14, 24.81 and 34.75 respectively. Interestingly the couple protection rate is slightly higher among the Christians than the other two sections of the tribe.

The high couple protection rate among the Christian Saura is due to the impact of the continued advise of the Christian Missionaries.

DISEASE

The scientific study of the disease is known as epidemiology. A considerable portion of tribal population is killed by different kinds of diseases. In the present paper, an attempt has been made to describe regarding the prevalance of various common diseases among the three sections of the tribe and how do they combat with them have also been discussed. Table 2.14 shows the various diseases found in different months of a year in this area.

TABLE 2.14: DISTRIBUTION OF COMMON DISEASES IN THE STUDY AREA

Months	*Name of the Diseases*
Jan-Mar	Asthama, Malaria, Skin disease, Respiratory trouble, Viral fever.
Apr-June	Malaria, Dysentery, Eye disease, Skin diseases.
July-Sept.	Malaria, Cold Fever, Diarrhoea, Cold cough.
Oct.Dec.	Malaria, Asthama, Respiratory trouble.

Source: Chandragiri Primary Health Centre.

Table 2.14 shows the common diseases during a Calendar year. Besides the above diseases, Tuberculosis, Sycosis, measles, etc., are also found among the people at the area. These people normally referred to their village medicine man or the Priest (Shaman) for their common ailments. But when the case is beyond the control of the traditional medicine man they come to the Primary Health Centre at Chandragiri. The Lanjia and the Sudha are not much conscious of their health and sanitation. On the other hand, the Christian missionaries educate the Christian Saura about the health and sanitation. They also provide free treatment and distribute medicines, baby foods and certain other commodities to the Christian

Saura. This has greatly helped the Christian Saura to become conscious of their health and sanitation.

MORTALITY

Mortality also determines the size of population and its composition by sex and age. According to the United Nations "Mortality is the percentage of death in the population". Mortality in the three sections of the tribe during one year prior to study has been discussed below. Table 2.15 shows the distribution of current deaths of the three sections of the Saura tribe.

TABLE 2.15 DISTRIBUTION OF CURRENT DEATHS OF THE SAURA TRIBE

Sections of Saura	*Male*	*Female*	*Total*	*C.D.R. (per 1000)*
Lanjia	15 (20.00)	13 (17.33)	28 (37.33)	26.00
Sudha	11 (14.70)	13 (17.33)	24 (32.00)	23.74
Christian	11 (14.70)	12 (16.00)	23 (30.66)	22.59
Total	37 (49.33)	38 (50.66)	75 (100)	

The crude death rate (C.D.R.) calculated from the above data among the Lanjia, the Sudha and the Christian Sauras are 26.60, 23.74, and 22.58 respectively. It is observed that more Lanjia males (20%) died last year than the females (17.33). But in case of Sudha and Christain Sauras more females 17.33% and 16% died in the same year respectively. However, the overall health situation among the Saura villages are not satisfactory in spite of the Government and Missionary efforts to overcome the health hazards of the Saura community as a whole.

CONCLUSION

In the present study it is observed that whatever changes have come to the Sauras are mostly due to the influence of Hindu and Christian religions. The two influential religions have a contrasting approach for changing the tribal culture. In Saura case, the acceptance of Hindu religion was possible due to a constant and continuous interaction among the Lanjia Saura and the neighbouring Hindu castes. This was an automatic process. No formal agents were necessary for the changes. This process is called as 'Hinduization'. However, for the acceptance of the Christianity the role of missionaries (agents of change) is unavoidable. Without the help of the missionaries the spread of Christianity would not have been possible. So in the former case it was automatic and in the later case it was organised. It would therefore be scientific to name the first type as 'Hinduization' and the second type as de-tribalization.

Whatever the process and the degree of change may be, in both cases, the Sauras are exposed to the greater world. Some of their blind and harmful practices are changed. Better economic and health care systems have gradually been accepted. Interest for education have culminated and above all new developmental thoughts have channelized. Therefore, any change which brings development and prosperity without hampering the national interest is good and should be acceptable to every family and community as a whole. Thus the tribes of India experienced the good and bad aspects of change. They are still in a fluid state and are anxiously waiting with their minds and hearts open to receive the light of the new socio-economic order.

REFERENCES

Agrawal, S.N. (1973) *India's population problem*, Bombay, pp. 86-93.

Ali Syed Ashfaq (1973) *Tribal Demography in Madhya Pradesh*, Jai Bharat Publishing House, Bopal, pp. 146-59.

Barclay, W.G (1958) *Technique of Population Analysis,* U.S.A.

Behura, N.K. (1990) "Tribal Societies in Orissa", *Tribes of Orissa*, Harijan and Tribal Welfare Deptt., Orissa, Bhubaneswar, pp. 10-21.

Das, N.C. (1979) "Demographic Aspects of the Gonds 1961-71", *Man in India*, Vol. 59, No-3, pp. 218-34.

Das, N.C. (1979) Fertility study of a Jung Village, *The Eastern Anthropologist*, Vol. 32, No. 3, pp. 185-91.

Das, N.C. and Pattnaik, P. (1985) Comparative Demographic Analysis between the Traditional and Hinduized Saura. *Adivasi*, vol. 24, No. 3 and 4, , pp. 18-24.

Elwin, V. (1955) *The Religion of an India Tribe.* Oxford University Press, Bombay.

Mohapatra, L.K. and Das, N.C. (1977) Social Structure and Demography of the Tribes of Orissa. *Tribal Problems of Today and Tomorrow.* Edt. P.C. Mohapatro and D. Panda, pp. 9-18.

Mamoria, C.B. (1957) *Tribal Demography of India,* Kitab Mahal, Allahabad.

Mohapatra, G. (1983) "Saora View of Good Life and Development", *Adivasi*, Vol. 23, No. 2, pp. 30-44.

Mohanty, B.B. (1990) "The Saora", *Tribes of Orissa*, T.R.W. Deptt. Orissa, Bhubaneswar, pp. 245-54.

Panda, C.D. (1989) "A study of couple fertility in a Tribal population of M.P.", *Population Transition in India*, Edt. S.N. Singh and others.

Patel, S. (1993) *Tribal Families and Fertility at Cross Road*, Delhi, pp. 57-68.

Patnaik, U.N. (1963-64) "Saoras of Ganjam Hills", *Adivasi*, Vol. 5, No. 1, pp. 6-13.

Patnaik, T. (1990) "The Sabara", *Tribes of Orissa*, Harijan and Tribal Welfare Department, Orissa, Bhubaneswar, pp. 255-60.

Tara Kanitkar, Ramesh B.M. and others (1994) *National Family Health Survey*, I.I.P.S., Bombay.

3

Socio-Economic and Cultural Life of the Kandhas of Kandhmal District: Orissa

Dr. Srikanta Mahapatra

The Kandhas are the original inhabitants of Kandhmal. They constitute 40.2 per cent of the total population of the district. Most of these Kandhas are away from urbanisation. The Kandhas are an aboriginal tribe of Orissa, speaking Kui language. The Kandhas inhabit the district in large number in spite of the precarious nature of their environment and shifting of their residence from place to place. They are a race of primitive people who were formerly used to bows and arrows for hunting for their livelihood. They are also a war-like tribe. Depending on the surrounding nature, the Kandhas of Kandhmal lead a different life-pattern from the Kandhas of other districts. Even though we notice some similarity among the Kandhas of the different districts, we notice marked dissimilarities in their customs, manners and culture. From the social point of view, the Kandhas can be grouped under 3 types—(1) Desia Kandha, (2) Dangaria Kandha, (3) Kutia Kandha, but all Kandhas in general are simple, truthful, skilful in work, faithful, courageous and highly

* *Dr. Mahapatra belongs to the faculty of Political Science, Adivasi College, Balhiguda (Orissa).*

hospitable. They depend on nature completely—nature with all her vagaries. As they live in valleys, hills and mountains covered with dense forests, they have to make the land arable. They clear the forest and then grow turmeric, 'ragi', 'Kandul' (Cow-pea), 'Janha', 'Binse' in the sloppy lands on the hills and mountains and at the foot of the hill they grow paddy, green ground nuts, black gram, mustard, horse-seed and vegetables. Their agricultural implements include plough, yoke, 'mahi' (the wooden ladder-leveller), spade, Khurupi and crow-bar, etc. The Kandhas of Kandhmal engage cows in cultivating the land. They also collect forest produce for their own use and sell the surplus, if any, in the nearby market.

The Kandhas live on ragi, tamarind seeds, roots and fruits of the forest and on the flesh of animals and birds, the stones of mangoes and on the root of 'salap tree'. They roast the raw flesh for their dish. They powder the soft inner part of mango stones and the soft inner part of the 'salap' tree, boil the powder in the way rice is done and eat it. But during festivals and ceremonies they feast on the flesh of domestic animals and birds such as goats, pigs, hens, etc. The Kandhas are very fond of wine and it is known as 'Kalu' in the Kandhmal district and 'Kedu' in the Koraput district. They can live on wine alone for days together. They prepare wine out of the juice of the 'Salap' tree or the flowers of the 'Mohua' tree or from rice. This tribe is so addicted to wine that it does not give up wine even if they are threatened with physical and mental torture, insult, loss of dignity and other damages. ·

The Kandha villages are mostly situated near forests and they habitually carry with them weapons such a 'tangis' (pick axes) or bow and arrows. With a tangi, a Kandha can fell a huge tree and can confront and overcome wild beasts, such as tigers and bears. The Kandha villages are extremely beautiful and enchanting to look at. They live in houses made of wooden walls and split bamboos, with a thatching of jungle grass and leaves of date-palm. There is generally an enclosure round the house for keeping away wild animals. The rooms are generally small and low-roofed. But each house has a raised verandah in the front, where men and women sit on their small 'charpaies', smoke, chitchat and spend their leisure and receive friends. The houses of the villages are generally constructed at the foot of a hill or mountain and a belt of evergreen mango, jack fruit, salap, mohua, etc., trees surrounds the village. No straight road runs through the village, nor are houses build in a file. Here and there we find the houses surrounded by boundaries made of bamboo and twigs. The walls are mostly made of clay, bamboo and twigs plastered together with wooden planks and wooden pillars. The floor of the house is usually smeared with the mixture of cowdung, water and the ashes of straw which looks hard and beautiful. Cowsheds are usually constructed by the side of the house.

The Kandhas occupy the whole of Kandhmal and the neighbouring states. They are short-statured, thick-nosed, flat-faced mongol-coloured (the colour varying from dark to yellow). The Kandha male is usually strong and stout and the Kandha female is healthy, tidy and beautiful to look at. The female is rather dwarfish, in stature and the cloth that she wears remains just above the knee. The Kutia or Dangaria Kandha male wears cloth that usually entwines the waist and one side of the cloth hangs on the front side while the other end of the cloth hangs on his back side. The female is fond of ornaments in general and the Kandha females of the Balliguda Sub-division, in particular are very fond of ornaments. They tatoo their faces beautifully and wear several aluminium, brass, or bell-metal rings on their ear-lobes by puncturing them. A female who has not done this is not considered eligible for marriage. At the age of ten or twelve the Kandha female is made unconscious with heavy drinks of wine and her face is tatooed. This becomes a very painful process and after tatooing, the face of the female swells enormously. She has to suffer severely for about a month. There are specific professionals who tatoo faces. The practice of tatooing is gradually waning with the spread of education and civilization in the district.

(2) KANDHA MARRIAGE

The marriage rites of the Kandhas are very funny. In this society, not the bride's side but the bridegroom's side gives dowry and this dowry is known as bride-price or 'ganthi'. In the remote past, giving bride-gold to the bride was in vogue and that has now degenerated into the present abominable dowry system. At the present in the Kandha society the bridegroom's side gives to the bride's side the bride-price consisting mostly of buffaloes, cows, oxen, metal pitcher and a little amount of money. The Kandha maidens and bachelors are allowed to mix freely as a result of which the Kandha youth gets a chance to select his or her own bride or bridegroom. The parents of the bridegroom, after being intimated their son's desire (they usually know it from the other youth of the village), send marriage proposals to the bride's parents. The 'Kendara' of the village who belongs to a Scheduled Caste, is sent to the bride's house to give the marriage proposal. Some days after that the elders of the bridegroom go to the bride's house to settle the date and condition of marriage. The elders of the bride and bridegroom with the help of mediators determine the quantity of the bride-price in their own traditional manner. The mediator of the bride's side brings in a basket ('Sewra' or 'grandua') stone, clay 'denuas', chips of broken earthen pitcher (Khapara) and bits of tree bark. Stone symbolises buffalo; clay 'denua' or 'dhenkala' symbolises ox; chips of broken pot symbolise metal pitchers. This basket is placed before both the sides. Different items are counted separately. Obviously the bride side, through this process, conveys to the bridegroom's side the number of each item that it wants from the other side. For example, if the bride's side keeps in the basket two stones, three earthen 'denuas', twenty chips of a broken earthen pot and four bits of bark, it indicates that they want two buffaloes, three oxen, twenty rupees and four metal pitchers. If the bride groom's side does not agree with the quantity of these items or if it thinks that giving these things of such quantity is beyond their means, then they retain in the basket such number of token things belonging to each category as they want to give actually and take out from the basket the surplus tokens. If the bride's side is not satisfied with the offer they increase the number of the tokens which may be less than the first demand. This bargain is repeated several times, if it is so needed. Finally, the mediators and the respectable men decide the quantity of demand basing on the ability of the bridegroom's side. After everything is settled regarding marriage, the wine pitcher is brought by the bridegroom's side, it is placed before the gathering. First it is offered to the deities and to the souls of the ancestors. Then wine is given to the elders and thereafter everybody else partakes of the wine. Then comes the turn of the bride's side. Their wine is distributed among all and the bride's side gives supper. Next day morning the bridegroom's side returns to its own village and on the appointed day, the bridegroom is led to the bride's house in a procession amidst songs and music. They carry with them the bride-price which consists of buffaloes, oxen, cows and money. In addition to that two pitchers full of wine are also taken. On their arrival, the bride's hamlet becomes quite festive and warm. Both the sides exchange traditional greetings and enjoy each others company. The brides side welcomes the bridegroom with much affection, takes him inside the home, smears his body with oil, turmeric paste of different dyes and also makes fun at his cost. Even the middleclass Kandha families make the bridegroom wear a new cloth and a golden necklace. If the bride's side is poor then it makes the bridegroom wear at least a silver armlet. The bridegroom's side also gives the bride a silver 'Khagata' to wear or make the bride wear a new saree. Both the bride and bridegroom show respect to the elders. The bride-side gives a feast that night and usually some domestic animals are killed for this feast. Next day the bridegroom's side along with the bridegroom return to their village assuring the bride-side the remaining portion of the bride-price, if any, as fixed earlier. Thereafter male persons of the bride-side visit the bridegroom's village and collect all that was to be given to the bride. There the marriage day is ascertained within two or three months. A few days before the marriage the friends of the bridegroom go to the bride's village to finalise the arrangements and they return home after being treated with feast and entertainment. On the day of marriage, the male members of the bridegroom-side dress the bridegroom in the bridegroom's attire. They tie horns to his head, making him hold bow, arrows and tangi. Then they carry the bridegroom one after another and proceed towards the bride's house with dance and music. On the other hand, the brothers, relatives of the bride make her wear a new dress and ornaments. Now both the bride and bridegroom are carried from the bride's house to the bridegroom's house. By this time arrangements are made in the bridegrooms house to receive both the bride and bridegroom with music, "Purna Kumbha' (an earthen pot filled with water and a coconut on the top of it—symbolic of good fortune) and 'deep' (a wick lighted with ghee in a flat earthen semi circular structure). This is also symbolic of sacredness, purity and good fortune. After their arrival, water is supplied to the persons of bride's side to wash their feet. In the meantime paddy is spread just outside the entrance of the house; and inside the entrance of it and a new cloth is covered over the paddy and rice. After the bride and bridegroom reach the spot, the bride is asked to walk over the new cloth and enter the house and that is how the marriage mostly ends. That day a sumptuous feast is given. The Kandhas drink a lot and dance a lot and enjoy the day of marriage. Here we notice that there is no necessity of marriage-altar or no necessity of the priest to do anything as is done in the non-tribal societies. Besides this, in the Kandha society, the 'Gandharba' system of marriage (marriage by elopement) is also in vogue. The bridegroom whose parents cannot afford to pay the bride-price abducts, with the help of his friends, his chosen bride from public places such as 'hat', fairs, bazars or functions and ceremonies and then marries her. Of course both the sides come to an amicable settlement after sometime of hot-tempers.

(3) THE FESTIVALS AND WORSHIPS OF KANDHAS

The different categories of tribals differ remarkably from one another in physical appearance, colour, language, customs, traditions and manners. But there is much in common among their festivals. Those festivals fall on specific time of the year and are differently named. The tribals live far away from the modern civilized society and as such the means of modern recreation have not reached them; the tribals enjoy themselves, during their festivals, with their own dance and music. They are so fond of the festive occasions that they borrow money from the money-lenders to meet festival expenses, at exorbitant rates of interest and have to repay the loan in kind by giving to the money lenders almost all their agricultural produce. For the rest of the year they have to live on the stone of the mangoes, the seeds of tamarind and various fruits of the forest. This practice has almost become hereditary. Beneath this wilful suffering, are their strong belief in God, religious rites and their conviction that God would give them enough to eat next year only if He is appeased. Like non-tribals, they celebrate the harvest ceremony and offer their new staple crop of the year (rice) to God and then partake of it. They ceremoniously offer God each of the crops they produce before partaking of it. That is one reason why the tribals have so many seasonal festivals with rituals conducted by their priests known as 'dehuri', 'Jhankara' or 'bedini'. One month before the festivals, these priest-like persons have to observe specific rules. They are not allowed to eat in other's houses; nor are they allowed to take fish, crab, meat and cakes; they are not also allowed to shave themselves or give their clothes to washerman to clean. They have the belief that mishaps take place in the rituals if the priest does not strictly adhere to the restrictions. The tribals almost worship the priest and obey his instructions very reverently. Some tribals have the custom to carry the priest on their shoulders to and from his house to the place of worship and back. At the time of worship the priest is given new clothes, paddy, rice, money, etc., as 'dakshina' (remuneration).

According to the Hindu scripture the month of 'margasir' is the first month of the year and on the last Thursday of this month the Kandhas and the Gondas, celebrate their Dalkhai festival. The worship of 'Anla' and Paddy plant is the remarkable feature of this festival. All the villagers go to the forest with their traditional music and gaiety and symbolically welcome and bring with them their God of that occasion. On that day goat, hen and other domestic animals are sacrificed and the people indulge in drink, feasts and merry-making. On the full-moon day of Pausa, the second month of the year, the Kandha and the Gonda tribals of Kalahandi district celebrate 'Pusa Puni' and on this occasion they worship their God, Mail. In some regions goats, hen, heifer and buffaloes are sacrificed by them. While sacrificing the buffaloes if the head of it, is not cut-off with the single stroke of the axe or sword, then they consider that entire year as inauspicious for them. The month of Magha, the third month of the year witnesses the celebration of 'Magha Parba' which is celebrated on a propitious day of the month. On that day the villagers with the priest fetch wood from the forest and at one end of the village build a hut. The priest sets fire to the hut after completing puja rituals. Then with cakes he is blind-folded, and the villagers move round the fire and throw into it different kinds of fruits, flowers and vegetables. After the end of this burn-fire they collect the baked and half-burned fruits and vegetables as the sacred prasad and ashes which they consider very sacred. Then they scatter them in their granaries and fields. They also hold a fest on that day. The next day the priest, after taking bath, goes to the burnt hut and scatters a handful of grains near the hut. The villagers till that land on which the grains are scattered. Domestic animals and birds are sacrificed once again and they hold a feast. Soon after the festival, the land is cleared of trees, shrubs and scrubs and they begin tilling the land and sowing seeds. This function is otherwise known as Magha Pudai. Then comes the month of Chaitra which is very sacred for the tribals and they celebrate Chaitra Parba. The Kandhas, Gonds, Sauras and some others celebrate the Kedu or Jhagadi festival in this month. With the pre-conception that mother earth wants to eat during this month. Previously human heads were sacrificed on this occasion and now buffaloes are being sacrificed. This is celebrated for five days at a stretch and on the last day the buffalo is sacrificed after several worship rites. The buffalo is tied to a strong sacrificial pole ('Jupa'). After being intoxicated with wine the tribals cut the flesh from the body of the live buffalo and bury that flesh in their respective fields. This was the way human beings had to suffer during the days of human sacrifice.

In 1845, the human sacrifice was abolished by the Government. And now, buffalo sacrifice is in vogue. The Parajas, Juangos, Juangos, Gadaba and Koya and some others of Koraput district also celebrate this festival. Dasahara is another major festival of the tribals and in this festival also domestic animals and birds are sacrificed. The highlights of different Kandha festivals are described hereunder.

(a) The Kedu Festival (The Podha Jatra)

The Kedu festival is one of the most important festivals of the Kandhas. Like all other tribals, the Kandhas hold their deity responsible for all mishaps in their society and they very unhesitantly sacrifice different domestic animals and birds to propitiate the God who they think, will ensure their safety. This festival is celebrated in the month of Baisakha and in Kandhmal District it is known as 'Jhagadi' festival. Mother-earth is worshipped during this festival. However, they also worship mountains, stones, trees, etc. The Kandhas have strong conviction that the propitiated mother earth will give them enough to eat and that She would prevent the outbreak of the fatal diseases such as Cholera, small-pox, etc. They also believe that She would save them from the attacks of the wild animals. The underlying motives of this festival is that the mother-earth wants to eat something like an animal. One year before the sacrifice of the buffalo, it is dedicated for sacrifice and is let out to graze freely. Even if it damages somebody's crops, it is not driven off the field and no complaint is made. Great care is taken of the animal and by the time of sacrifice the buffalo becomes very fat. In the past a human being was sacrificed. The Panas of the village abducted a human being and sold him to the Kandhas. Even on occasions they sold their children to be sacrificed. The person thus procured was known as Meria for which the Kandhas were to pay an amount ranging from Rs. 60/- to Rs. 200/-. To put an end to this barbarous inhuman and superstitious practice the British Government in 1845 appointed Capt. McFarson as the Special Agent. With the help of Mr. Campbell the former could put an end to this pernicious practice.

The Kandhas who celebrate this festival make their houses neat and clean two days before the actual festival and invite their guests. In Balliguda this festival is celebrated for five days. The priest who is to perform Puja rites has to observe certain restriction. He is not allowed to go to his relatives house and he is not allowed to take cake, fish, crabs, etc. The Puja begins on a Saturday. That day the villagers accompany the priest to the forest with the playing of different musical instruments and collect a tall bamboo after due Pujas. A little amount of turmeric, flower, unboiled rice and wine is used as the 'Puja' material. On the second day a 'Chatti' is tied to the top of the bamboo which is then fixed vertically in a hole on the ground. Then the villagers take bath, put on new garments, wash the buffalo with turmeric water and smear its head with oil, ghee and vermilion. Then they decorate its neck with garlands and a new cloth and take it to every villager's door-step. At every door-step the beast is worshipped and is fed with cakes of various kinds. It is then brought to the spot of sacrifice and to a pole, and near the pole a pig and a hen are first sacrificed. A little flesh of the sacrifices is then tied to the bamboo with a 'Chatti' on it. On the third day the buffalo is brought to the 'Meri' (Sacrificial pole). All other arrangements for sacrifice are made, the buffalo is made to lie on the ground forcibly with the villagers passing across the body of the lying buffalo. After performing the Puja, the priest or 'dehuri' pierces a spear three times into the belly of the beast and soon the villagers and the people of nearby villages start cutting flesh ravenously from the live buffalo, run with bits of flesh and burry them in their respective fields. While cutting flesh from the buffalo they are heavily drunk and through the bustle and hurry they sometimes injure each other's body—sometimes a hand is also cut off. And on that day a sumptuous feast is held in the village which is partaken of by the villagers and their guests. Where the festival runs for five days at a stretch, two buffaloes are sacrificed. After the festival the priest is given money, rice and clothes, etc., as 'dakshina'. The potter who had supplied earthern pitchers and the black-smith who had supplied 'tangi' and weapons and the professional people engaged in playing with musical instruments are duly rewarded. And the simple-minded tribals feel gratified after finishing the 'Puja' of their deity this way.

(b) Pituli Puja (Worship of idols)

The Kandhas are generally idol (Pituli) worshippers. After the plantation work is over they worship their agricultural instruments and cows and bullocks. They even decorate and worship the cowshed and sacrifice hens and eggs. The Kandhas who are in need of wealth to purchase 'Pitulies' and worship them. Inside the family they worship the idols secretly and also worship their village goddess with much faith which is known as 'Gram Debati' (goddess of their own village). In each month they perform Yangyns (sacred sacrificial fires) before her. They also offer eggs to their village goddess but the priest has only right to perform it. In the month of March the villagers assemble together and go in a procession towards their Kulada Bag Devi. There they sacrifice hens, goats and sheep and also give coconut and fruits. But they do it in the corner of the village. The Kandhas of Kandhmal also believe in Lord Siva, Bishnu and Laxmi. At the same time most of the Kandhas believe in ghosts and spirits as a result of which the witches get a chance to play a dominant role in the villages by uttering hymns to ward off the spirits. Witchcraft is mostly believed by the Kandhas.

(c) Burbi Puja (Worship of the goddess of earth)

The Kandhas of Kandhmal have strong faith in the earth Goddess. They call it 'Tadapenu' in the month of July. They observe this ceremony with great joy and at the time of this festival the villagers are gathered together and it is performed with the help of the Sarpanch. From each village one dance party is sent to the main spot. The spot is selected by the important persons and on that day all musical instruments like the dhol, the mardal, the turi, and the band, etc., are played there. By wearing horns on their heads they go to the spot in a procession. They follow the direction and instruction of the priest and dance the whole day with all formalities. It is very interesting and charming to look at the Kandhas during this dance who hold arrows, bows and pick axes which is known as 'tangi' in Kui language. In the meanwhile, the priest recities 'mantras' and after that they sacrifice sheep and goats and some people also offer coconuts and fruits. They believe that if the earth Goddess is pleased they will get enough food material.

(d) Marangi Puja

This puja is observed by the Kandhas of Kandhmal after plantation of paddy which is called 'marangi parba'. Just like the Baladeve puja or 'Gamha Purnima' of non-tribals, they observe this festival and from this day onwards they consume maize and other vegetables.

(e) Nuakhia

After harvesting the Kandhas of Kandhmal receive the new grain which is produced by them. They make merry and dance the whole day with all musical instruments and they (including boys and girls) drink very often. In each family they arrange a feast on the occasion of the Nuakhia. The name is so because on this day they begin taking new grains or paddy.

(f) Sadakoru Festival

The Kandhas of Kandhmal perform Sadakoru 'Jatra' in a new moon night of chilly winter. In this festival, they sacrifice a buffalo to pacify the ghosts of the forefathers of the Kandhas. They keep some wine along with the cooked buffalo meat in the graveyard. Dance is strictly prohibited in the night because of the frequent roaming of the ghosts in the village.

(g) Salang Festival

This is a private festival of the Kandha family of the Kandhmal district before going for sowing seeds. In the home itself, the head of the family keeps the seeds reserved in a basket for sowing. They put a hen inside the said basket with the purpose of killing it by twisting its neck. When it is killed, some blood of that hen mixes with the seeds. Then one egg is broken and its yolk is mixed with wine in a pot. Then everybody of the family generally touches the basket and proceeds towards the field. In the field, the head of the family first of all throws the egg mixed with wine, then they begin to sow.

(h) Dhankhod Festival

The Kandhas of Kandhmal perform this festival after reaping the products. Generally they store their agricultural products in a bamboo which is known as 'Dhankhod'. This puja is observed before keeping the grains inside it.

First of all the Dhankhod is cleaned and smeared with cow-dung, to avoid the insects from destroying the grains inside it. Then they throw a hen inside the Dhankhod and sprinkle wine on its floor and walls. The head of the family then fills the vessel with grains as a result of which the hen dies out of suffocation. So the spirit of the hen remains inside the vessel to guard the grains from being destroyed by rats and insects. Then the dead hen is removed and a home feast is arranged with its meat and wine.

(i) Dalkhai Puja (Laxmi Puja)

The Dalkhai dance is a famous festival dance of the Kandhas. At some places it is also known as Laxmi Puja. This falls on the last Thursday of Margasira and Paddy and 'Anla' are worshipped on this occasion. The worship of 'Anla' is symbolic of the worship of the forest deity. The caste Hindus worship mostly Siba and Vishnu but the tribals worship the various manifestations of nature such as the earth, mountain, stone, trees, etc. In their language the deity is known as 'Penu' and the puja is known as ' Laka'. Sarupenu, Tanapenu, Sugapenu and Pidupenu respectively mean the deity of mountain, the deity of earth and the deity of water and the dead forefathers.

The Kandhas celebrate, when the fields are rich with paddy, blackgram, 'Kandula', etc. They have the belief that they would have good harvest and that the danger of contagious diseases would be removed if they worshipped paddy and 'Anla'. The modern means of entertainment and recreation have scarcely entered the Kandha society and till now most of them have been celebrating their festivals in their old, original, traditional ways. The very remarkable feature is that during the festivals all the villagers and the people of the nearby villages immerse themselves deep into the mirth of the festivals. They invite their guests of the nearby villages two days in advance of the celebration of this festival. They make their houses neat and clean; they make themselves sacred by washing their clothes and by substituting old earthen pitchers by new ones for cooking. Next day the villagers decorate two goats by smearing vermilion on their heads and by garlanding them. Then they bring a pitcher filled with the paddy of the current year and place the pitcher on a new napkin kept forming a ring. All the male and female Kandhas fast that day and do 'bandapana' (offering of light) to pitcher with milk, unboiled rice, flower, vermilion and dhupa (scented smoke and deepa). In the evening the male members go to the forest with 'Chhatti', 'Tarasa', 'Music' in the midst of great joy. They take with them the pitcher, goats and other puja materials such as earthen pitcher and plate, tangi, muan (a confection made of fried rice and molasses), flower and vermilion. Prior to this, an 'Anla' tree near a rock is located and these people keep the puja materials and the pitcher on a rock. Once again 'bandapana' (Offering of light) is done to the pitcher. The potter unusually supplies newly made 'rukha' (lamp stand), lamp and 'baitha', etc. For the puja a priest is employed and he is assisted by another person known as 'bedini'. This 'dehuri', 'bedint' and the butcher are given a piece of new cloth each. In addition to this, each of them gets ten 'gounis' of paddy as their wages. This 'bedini' is otherwise a person known as 'Kalasi' or the temporary foreteller. When asked he foretells about the future state of affairs of the people, cows, oxen and their diseases, etc. And people sincerely believe what he foretells. After sometime he stops foretelling and becomes senseles and his sense is revived by splattering water to his face. Of the two goats brought for puja one is brought to the villagers and they throw on the goat unboiled rice, flower and 'bel' leaves, etc. Wishing their own welfare they fall flat before their deity. Then the goat is sacrificed, its flesh is cooked and after taking its flesh they spend the night there. Next day, that is on Thursday, about 12 a.m. they worship the 'Anla' tree, the paddy plant and the pitcher containing the paddy. Milk is brought from the village for worship. All people of the village making music, dancing and drinking. All of them carry an 'Anla' twig and a paddy plant each. The remaining persons of the village welcome these people mid-way with music. This is known as Dalkhai welcome. People of the nearby village also join them. After returning, they move round the Dalkhai temple seven times and erect in front of the 'guda' house (Dalkhai temple) 'Chhati' and 'trasas' (types of umbrellas). Then the pitcher filled with milk is kept in the God's room. In the evening they worship the God with turmeric powder, unboiled rice and other Puja materials. By 10 to 11 p.m. the Puja ends. Here also a person automatically becomes a 'Kalasi'—temporary foreteller and answers questions regarding future. The remaining goat (the second one) is sacrificed and the Kandhas return dancing to their village with the sacrificed goat and other things. The paddy pitcher is then kept in the priest's house and the villagers preserve their own paddy plants in their own homes with great care. That day the festival is concluded with a sumptuous feast.

(J) Danda Nach (Meru Jatra)

The Kandhas of Kandhmal are the devotees of Lord Siva. To get blessing from him for their sons and daughters, they perform

Danda Nach. From each family one member is interested to take part in it. In the month of April, the ceremony continues for thirteen days. Here, one member of the family prays and fasts in the day time and it has similarity with that of the Danda Nach of Ganjam District. During these days they move from village to village and even dance on the hot sand and beside the burning fire. In the night time the people arrange the dance in different villages for all these days and ultimately on the 13th day they conclude the ceremony which is known as ' Meru Jatra'.

ECONOMIC LIFE OF KANDHAS

(i) Hunting

Hunting is one of the traditional occupations of Kandhas. Their hunting weapons are bows, arrows and axes. The Kandhas are very fond of hunting deer, Sambar, 'Kutra' (wild Boar) and other wild animals and birds. They hunt the birds by a sharp iron arrow which is locally made. Even though restrictions have been imposed on hunting by the Forest Department, still then the Kandhas have not yet completely abandoned the practice.

(ii) Liquor

From birth to death, liquor plays a very important role in the Kandha society. They are very much fond of liquor and also drink regularly. They use three kinds of liquor, such as : (i) Pranga Kalu or Fatul Moda—prepared from rice and Koir. (ii) Madang—Collected from Khajuri or Salap Mada. (iii) Anking or Puji—Mahuli Mada distilled from Mohua flower.

The following are the reasons for which the Kandhas are addicted to drinking from their birth to death.

(1) Liquor is used both as a preventive and curative medicine. It is believed that by drinking liquor a Kandha is cured from cold, headache and pains.

(2) It is used to mitigate conflicts.

(3) It has high social value. The guest and relatives are entertained by it.

(4) In festivals and dances it is highly essential.

(5) It removes tensions from the mind and gives sound sleep.

(6) In times of want and food scarcity, they take liquor to be relieved of hunger for days together.

(7) It has religious and social significance in marriages.

(8) It is highly required for rituals. In rituals and festivals liquor is offered to the ancestors and deities to get their blessings and to keep them well.

(9) It creates and sustains friendship. A leaf-cup of liquor is a medium of social inter-course.

(iii) Forest Produce

The life of the Kandha is linked with forest. Apart from the agricultural produces they collect minor forest produce such as tamarind, mango, mohua flowers and seeds, broom grass, honey, gums, Kendu leaf, Siali leaf, Sal seed, Harida, Bahada, Anla, various kinds of roots and fruits and medicinal herbs, etc. The forest is also the source of timber, bamboo, fire wood, etc., for their household necessities.

Kandhas take up animal husbandry as a subsidiary occupation. They keep cows, ploughing bullocks, goats, sheep, pigs and poultry birds. Cattle force is applied in agriculture. Of course at the time of need they sell their surplus goats and pigs and get some money. Even during wants they never hesitate to part their cows and bullocks for a few bucks. They offer cows, bullocks, goats and pigs as Gonthi (Dowry) during marriages. They also kill goats, sheep, pigs and poultry birds for their consumption.

SHIFTING CULTIVATION

The primary economic activity of the tribal folk is cultivation of land by primitive methods. The Kandhas practise the primitive system of shifting cultivation locally known as 'Podu' cultivation in the hill tracts, which is an age old practice of the tribals. As the name indicates, they fell trees on slopes of mountains and after the felled trees dry up they set fire to them. When it is reduced to ashes they scratch up the burnt ashes and cultivate the land. Thus in this system a plot of land is not regularly cultivated year after year, rather the cultivator shifts or moves from one plot to another at two to three years interval and hence the name 'Shifting Cultivation'.

LIFE CYCLE

(a) Birth Rite

It is a belief among the Kandhas that a person passes through five stages in his life—infancy, childhood, adolescence, adulthood and old age. After the marriage, if the pair is blessed with a son or daughter, they happily spend the time. During one month of Child's birth, the mother and the child remain aloof in a separate room. The mother does not touch any body and no body enters that secluded room. Even other family members do not touch the lady who has given birth, except her husband. Just after 30 days, full purificatory rites are observed. On this occasion the clan members and also the relatives by marriage take part in the rituals. A feast is prepared and the assembled relatives and kin members are offered food and drink. They carry the child with a large procession, which is known as "Adeki Sadapadina". Now-a-days the educated Kandhas are performing the 'Annual Birth Days' of their children.

Puberty Rite

When a grown up girl in Kandha society becomes mature or attains puberty, then it is celebrated. The ceremony for this is called 'Sirududa' or 'Dinadibd'. On this occasion the family members give a new cloth to the girl. She remains aloof from the family members and after a week the girl comes out and mixes with her friends and girls of her own age.

Death Rites

It is believed by the Kandhas that life and death are determined by the Supreme Being, Dharani Penu who has created this world. After death of a person the dead body is carried by the family members and by the neighbours of the street. They take it through the back side of the house to the burial ground. The eldest son always sets fire to the dead body of his father by lighting a bundle of straw and then thrusting it into the pyre. Then others follow him. Until the body is cremated entirely, it is watched, lest it may become ghost in future. The next day again they go to the burial ground with an axe and all the things that were used by the person who is dead and keep all the used things of the dead on the burial ground. After returning from that place they give information to their relatives. On the 5th Day from the day of death, for purification of their soul, that is 'Sudhi', they arrange a feast. Relatives, community members and neighbours are invited on this occasion to participate in this feast. The same tradition is followed in case of a young man's death but they do not perform these things when a body is dead. In case of a baby's death they simply go and bury him in a burial ground. As the Kandhas of Kandhmal do not get ample health facilities and have hygienic conditions around them, their death rate is very high. Moreover, during natural calamities like cholera and malaria, it becomes unmanageable.

Belief-System Regarding Diseases and Traditional Methods of Treatment

The Kandhas of Kandhmal areas generally believe in the prevalence of benevolent and malevolent spirits which influence the life in many ways. The most important functionary which concerns us most in the context of health culture is the witch doctor, who is called 'Kutaka' or ' Bejuni'. The witch-doctor knows the techniques of counter-acting the evil effects of black magic and appeases the malevolent spirit which cause disease and death. The Kandha also follow several taboos concerning social and religious customs. They also believe that any breach of such taboos causes illness and death.

According to their thinking if a Kandha child is suffering from chicken pox or measles, it is due to the anger of their Dharani Penu (village goddess). To cure the disease they hardly go to hospital and both the mother and the child observe certain religious taboos. Besides, they worship at the shrine of Dharani Penu and after which it is presumed that the child would recover from the disease.

Some Suggestions for the Development of the Kandhas

1. Government should take proper steps to develop transport, postal, railway, telegraph, telephone, television facilities in tribal areas for their modernization.

2. To develop educational facilities, one residential Ashram School in every Panchayat and one Residential High School in every Panchayat should be set up by the Government.

3. Thirdly, in Kandhmal district high calibre, honest, sincere, efficient and other desirable officers shall be posted to protect the interest of the tribals.

4. Fourthly, the forest Department should create sufficient employment opportunities through the Forest Co-operatives and Afforestation Programmes and associate Kandhas in conserving the environment.

5. Fifthly, Government should teach them by various agencies the modern and improved agricultural practices. Modern agricultural tools and machines shall be demonstrated in the Kandhmal district to make them realise about their benefits.

6. Sixthly, the Kandhas are exploited by the private money lenders by paying exorbitant rates of interest and by many dishonest means. To save the Kandhas from the clutches of the money lending sahukars the Government has to provide alternative means of credit to the Kandhas.

7. Seventhly, Minor Irrigation Project shall be established in Kandhmal areas which is a dire need of the people.

REFERENCES

1. The Kandha of Orissa by N. Pattnaik, P.S. Das Pattnaik, THRTI, 1982.
2. The Phulbani District Gazetter.
3. The Kandhas of Phulbani—by Sasibhusan Tiyadi
4. The Culture of Phulbani District, Maguni Dash.

4

Some Aspects of Tribal Development in Orissa

C.R. Dash*

The concept of development embraces all aspects of life and activity, with a goal to enrich the quality of life and ensure its availabiity at minimum levels to all sections of the population. In fact, development is not merely the provision of opportunities for resource development in the light of appropriate science and technology but also their utilisation, thus, implies the creation of the necessary facilities for such utilisation. Therefore, the power structure, its class composition and its unequal incidence in the interests it serves, institutions—economic, social and political—the state of the law, the state of knowledge and use of science and technology, information and communication, attitude, monitoring and evaluating the progress of development—all these fall within the scope of development. Development is no longer the exclusive concern of the professional economist or scientist or technologist but becomes an inter-disciplinary concept.

Galbraith considered 'effective government, education and Social Justice as critically important for advancement of a country

* *Economic Research Supervisor, NKC Centre for Development Studies, Chandrasekharpur, Bhubaneswar (Orissa)*

and diagnosing barrier to advance is of critical importance. And it follows that until these barriers are removed little will come from capital investment and technical assistance. While plans will be big in paper they will be small in result. (Galbraith).

In order to achieve development the duty of state, as stated in Directive Principles of state policy in the constitution of India that "State will promote with special care the educational and economic interest of the weaker section and in particular of the Scheduled Caste and Scheduled Tribes and shall protect them from all forms of exploitation". Therefore, the concept of growth with Social Justice is said to be basic the philosophy of development underlying Indian economic planning.

METHODOLOGY

Therefore, in this background the tribals of Orissa and their demographic feature, various aspects of development are examined in this paper by the help of taking census figures, reports, survey results, of Government of India, Government of Orissa, academic studies, studies of reputed Organisations and data from reliable secondary sources.

CONCEPT OF SCHEDULED TRIBE AND CENSUS

The Census organisation of India in 1901, under direction of Sir Herbert Risley had done some pioneering work on the Tribal Communities in India. In 1931, Dr. J.H. Hulton, the then Census Commissioner of India seriously pursued to enlist the primitive tribes at the census of 1931. In pre-Independence era for the first time in the Government of India Act, 1935 a reference was made to the 'backward tribes'. As per the 13th schedule to the Government of India order of 1936, some of the tribes were identified as backward. After India won her independence, the Constitution of India under Article 46 reads as "The State shall promote with special care the educational and economic interests of the weaker sections of the people and in particular, of the Scheduled Castes and Scheduled Tribes and shall protect them from Social Justice and all forms of exploitation". As per Article 342, the Scheduled Tribes 'are tribes or the tribal communities or ports of or groups within tribes or tribal communities'. Under Article 339, the President shall appoint a

Commission at the expiry of ten years from its commencement to report on the administration of what are known as the scheduled areas and the welfare of the Scheduled Tribes in the states.

The list of Scheduled Tribes was first notified by the President of India in 1950 and modified in 1956 listed 62 Scheduled Tribes in Orissa. According to 1991 Census there are 70,32,214 Scheduled Tribes population in Orissa constituting 22.21 per cent of the total population of the state.

SCHEDULED TRIBE POPULATION IN ORISSA

The Scheduled Tribe population in Orissa constituted about 24.07 per cent of total population in 1961 census. But subsequent census figures revealed that the proportion of S.T. population declined in comparison to total population. Table 4.1 depicts the figures of total population, S.T. population and percentage of S.T. population to total population from 1961 to 1991. The percentage of S.T. population to total population in 1961, 1971, 1981 and 1991 were 24.07%, 23.11%, 22.43% and 22.21 per cent respectively.

TABLE 4.1: PERCENTAGE OF SCHEDULED TRIBE POPULATION TO TOTAL POPULATION OF ORISSA FROM 1961 TO 1991.

Sl. No.	*Year*	*Total population*	*S.T. population*	*Percentage of S.T. population to total population*
1	2	3	4	5
1.	1961	17,548,846	42,23,757	24.07
2.	1971	21,944,615	50,71,937	23.11
3.	1981	26,370,271	59,15,067	22.43
4.	1991	31,659,736	70,32,214	22.21

Source: Compiled from various series of 'Census of India', Jomaganana Bhawan Library, Orissa.

DECADAL GROWTH RATE OF S.T. POPULATION

It is pertinent to note that the declining proportion of S.T. population to total population is due to low relative decadal growth rate of S.T. population in Orissa since 1961 to 1991. The percentage growth of population is depicted in Table 4.2.

TABLE 4.2: DECADAL GROWTH OF ST AND SC POPULATION

Sl. No.	*Period*	*Percentage of S.T. population*	*Growth of S.C. population*	*Total population*
1	2	3	4	5
1.	1961-71	20.08	19.79	25.05
2.	1971-81	16.62	16.75	20.17
3.	1981-91	18.89	32.69	20.06

Source: Compiled from Various 'Census publications'.

It is pertinent to note from Table 4.2 that the per cent of growth of S.T. population is much slower as compared to the growth rate of total population of Orissa. Barring 1961-71 per cent of growth of S.T. population remained lower than the growth of S.C. population of the state. It also shows the growth rate of S.T. population for the decades 1961-71, 1971-81 and 1981-91 is 20.08 per cent, 16.62 per cent and 18.89 per cent respectively whereas rate of growth of S.C. population for the same period shows 19.79 per cent, 16.75 per cent and 32.69 per cent as against growth rate of 25.05 per cent, 20.17 per cent and 20.06 per cent in case of total population of Orissa during the corresponding three decades.

LITERACY RATE OF S.T.

Education is basic input for development of human being. Without proper education it is beyond imagination to develop challenge to the Scheduled Tribes encounter. Now is the question for overall development through education through which development issues relating to economic, cultural, health, nutrition, etc., can be effectively communicated. The basic impact of education on tribals particularly women, will have bearing on increasing the standard of living of household, reduction of fertility rate, and improvement of health and nutritional status at the household level.

But the literacy rate of S.T. population is lower than state population.

The census figures of 1961,1971,1981 and 1991 depicted in Table 4.3 revealed that the literacy rate in Orissa was 25.24 per cent, 30.53 per cent, 40.96 per cent and 49.09 per cent whereas Tribal literacy rate for the corresponding period were 7.36 per cent, 9.46 per cent, 13.96 per cent and 22.31 per cent respectively, which showed considerably like the Scheduled Caste literacy rate of 11.57 per cent, 15.61 per cent, 22.41 per cent and 36.78 per cent respectively for the same period. In case of literacy rate of tribals in Orissa increased both in percentage and absolute numbers but that of consistent inequality in literacy rate persisting throughout the decade comparatively from other social groups.

TABLE 4.3 LITERACY RATE OF S.T., S.C. AND ALL POPULATION IN ORISSA

Census Year	*Population*	*S.T.*	*S.C.*	*All*
1961	Persons	7.36	11.57	25.24
	Male	13.04	19.82	40.26
	Female	1.77	3.44	10.12
1971	Persons	9.46	15.61	30.53
	Male	16.38	15.98	44.50
	Female	2.58	5.17	16.29
1981	Persons	13.96	22.41	40.96
	Male	23.27	35.26	46.45
	Female	4.76	9.40	25.14
1991	Persons	22.31	36.78	49.09
	Male	34.44	52.42	63.09
	Female	10.21	20.74	34.68

Source: Compiled from various "Census of India"— Orissa publications.
N.B. In 1991 census all Children below age 7 years have been treated as illiterates. In 1961, 1971 and 1981 Census all children below 5 were treated as illiterates.

While the percentage of illiteracy among the total population is the principal index of the level of education in a country, the relationship between figures for each sex becomes an index of equality of men and women (UNESCO, 1970). Female literacy has an important bearing on scoio-economic condition of society. Unless women are educated, there is little scope for the socio-economic transformation of the society (Mangat, 1994). Therefore, in order to analyse the socio-economic progress of tribal society sex-wise literacy rates is depicted in Table 4.3 from 1961 to 1991. The percentage of literacy for males and females were 40.26 and 10.12 in 1961, 44.50 and 16.29 in 1971, 46.45 and 25.14 in 1981 and in 1991 the percentage of literacy for males 63.09 whereas for females it was 34.68 in the State of Orissa. The tribal literacy in Orissa for males and females were 13.04 per cent and 1.77 per cent in 1961, 16.38 per cent and 2.58 per cent in 1971, 23.27 per cent and 4.76 per cent in 1981 and 34.44 per cent and 10.21 per cent in 1991 respectively. Male and Female literacy rate in case of tribals indicate slower progress than the Scheduled Caste literacy rate.

TABLE 4.4: SEX RATIO IN ORISSA FOR S.T., S.C. AND ALL SOCIAL GROUPS FROM 1961 TO 1991 (FEMALES PER 1000 MALES)

Sl. No.	*Social Groups*	*1961*	*1971*	*1981*	*1991*
1	2	3	4	5	6
1.	S.T.	1016	1007	1012	1002
2.	S.C.	1015	993	988	975
3.	All social groups	1001	988	981	971

Sex-Ratio : Sex ratio expressed in numbers of female population per 1000 males depicted in Table 4.4. In 1961 sex ratio was positive particularly for S.T. and S.C population in Orissa. In case of Orissa, Sex ratio has declined from 1001 in 1961 to 1988 in 1971, 981 in 1981 and 971 in 1991. The sex ratio for S.T. population, however, was 1016 in 1961 declined to 1007 in 1971 then improved in 1981 to 1012 and again reduced tc 1002 in 1991. Despite declining sex ratio for the state population including S.C., S.T. population showing positive sex ratio speaks a volume for itself.

WORK FORCE PARTICIPATION

The work force participation of Scheduled Tribe population in Orissa is unfolded in Table 4.5. Total main workers constitute 53.94 per cent in 1961, 34.80 per cent in 1971, 39.78 per cent in 1981 and 40.24 per cent in 1991 of S.T. population. Due to change in concept of work and classification of workers 1981 and 1991 work participation rate can be computed by adding main workers and marginal workers. Segregated figures on the basis of sex of workers explained male and female composition of workforce of the tribal population in Orissa from 1961 to 1991. But of total main workers, cultivators constituted 62.78 per cent, 53.52 per cent, 52.15 per cent and 50.82 per cent in 1961, 1971, 1981 and 1991 census whereas agricultural labourers constituted 22.22 per cent, 37.27 per cent, 36.21 per cent and 38.27 per cent for the respective periods. There has been marginal decline in per cent of cultivators and increase in agricultural laburers for tribals. Sex-wise distribution of workers further revealed from the data that the per cent of cultivators to total workers for males were 65.92 per cent, 59.10 per cent, 59.80 per cent and 58.65 per cent during 1961,1971,1981 and 1991 census whereas for the same period female cultivators constituted 58.28 per cent, 23.38 per cent, 29.24 per cent and 31.26 per cent respectively. The percentage distribution of workforce by sexes revealed that the per cent of male agricultural labourers constituted 21.09 per cent, 32.88 per cent, 29.10 per cent and 30.21 per cent in 1961,1971,1981 and 1991 census respectively whereas corresponding period figures for female workforce were 23.82 per cent, 60.93 per cent, 57.53 per cent and 58.37 per cent respectively.

TABLE 4.5: SEX-WISE DISTRIBUTION OF WORKERS AMONG S.T. POPULATION IN ORISSA FROM 1961 TO 1991

Sl. No.	*Sex*	*1961*	*1971*	*1981*	*1991*
1. Total Main workers and their percentage to total population	P	2,230,931 (53.94)	1,714,228 (34.80)	2,353,034 (39.78)	2,829,688 (40.24)
	M	1,306,756 (63.75)	1,446,184 (58.99)	1,764,306 (60.01)	2,020,152 (57.51)
	F	924,175 (44.29)	2,68,044 (10.84)	588,728 (19.79)	8,09,536 (16.73)
2. Cultivators and their percentage to total workers	P	1,400,667 (62.78)	917,426 (53.52)	1,227,195 (52.15)	1,437,919 (50.82)
	M	862,072 (65.92)	854,765 (59.10)	1,055,067 (59.80)	1,184,837 (58.65)
	F	838,595 (58.28)	62,661 (23.38)	172,128 (29.24)	253,082 (31.26)
3. Agricultural labourers and their percentage to total workers	P	495,706 (22.22)	638.831 (37.27)	851,998 (36.21)	1,082,907 (38.27)
	M	275,604 (21.09)	475,514 (32.88)	513,329 (29.10)	610,373 (30.21)
	F	220,102 (23.82)	163,317 (60.93)	338,669 (57.53)	472,534 (58.37)
4. Marginal workers and their per centtage to total population.	P	-	-	570,318 (9.64)	641,662 (9.12)
	M	-	-	57,018 (1.94)	50,199 (1.43)
	F	-	-	513,300 (17.25)	591,463 (16.81)
5. Non workers and their total percentage to population	P	1,905,275 (46.06)	3,210,354 (65.19)	2,991,715 (50.58)	3,560,864 (50.64)
	M	742,997 (36.25)	1,005,239 (41.01)	1,118,539 (38.05)	1,442,540 (41.06)
	F	1,162,270 (55.71)	2,205,115 (89.16)	1,873,176 (62.96)	2,118,324 (60.19)

P=Person, M= Males, F= Females

Source: Compiled from various publications of Census of India, Orissa

Except 1961 Census the percentage of female workers classified as cultivators were around half of the per cent of male worker cultivators whereas agricultural labourers percentage figure showed female workers constituted around double the per cent of male agricultural labourers of the total female workers around 60 per cent classified as agricultural labourers is enough to explain how tribal women have been toiling to earn livelihood for their households. Again in 1981 and 1991 classification of workers as main and marginal workers showed per cent of female marginal workers were 17.25 and 16.81 whereas per cent of male workers classified as marginal workers for the same period were 1.94 per cent and 1.43 per cent respectively. There are several contributary factors for high marginal female workers of which the pivot factor responsible is restricted scope of work and employment.

NON-WORKERS

Various census enumeration revealed that the S.T. non-workers during 1961, 1971, 1981 and 1991 were 46.06 per cent, 65.19 per cent, 50.58 per cent and 50.64 per cent respectively. From 1961 census and onwards per cent of male non-workers fluctuated between 36.25 per cent in 1961 to 41.06 per cent in 1991 whereas female per cent of non-workers fluctuated from 89.16 per cent in 1971 to 60.19 per cent in 1991. The female per cent of non-workers has been higher than per cent of male non workers during all census conducted so far.

Table 4.6 depicts the number, area and average size of operation holding of S.Ts. in Orissa. It reveals that the number of marginal holdings increased from 3.8 lakhs in 1980-81 to 4.5 lakhs in 1985-86 and 5.1 lakhs in 1990-91 whereas number of large and medium size of holdings declined. So far as average size of operational land holding is concerned size of marginal holding declined from 0.6 hect. in 1980-81 to 0.5 hect. in 1985-86 and remained constant in 1990-91. Size of small holding remained constant from 1980-81 to 1990-91 at 1.4 hect. Operational holding size of tribals classified as semi-medium (from 2.0 hect, to 4.00 hect), however, improved from 2.6 hect in 1980-81 to 2.7 hect in 1985-86 and 1990-91. The average size of operational land holding of tribal medium from size (4.0 hect, to 10.0 hect) fluctuated from 5.5 hect in 1980-81 to 5.8 hect in 1985-86 and in 1990-91 It was reported only 5.0 hect. Large holding consist of 10.0 hect. and above, the average size of operational holding had been increasing from 13.2 hect in 1980-81 to 14.4 hect. in 1985-86 and it was 16.7 hect in 1990-91. The report of Agricultural Census Commissioner revealed that the total number of tribal operational holding in 1980-81, 1985-86 and 1990-91 were 9.2 lakhs 9.6 lakhs and 10.5 lakhs increased due to might be fragmentation and division of holding arose because of division of joint family and increasing population and households. But total area of operational holding reported 15.7 lakhs hect., 15.5 lakhs hect and 15.2 lakhs hect. in 1980-81, 1985-86 and 1990-91 respectively showed a declining trend and average size of operational holding declined, i.e., 1.7 acres, 1.6 acres and 1.4 acres for the same period.

TABLE 4.6: NUMBER, AREA AND AVERAGE SIZE OF OPERATIONAL HOLDING IN BROAD SIZE GROUP FOR SCHEDULED TRIBES IN ORISSA. (NO. IN LAKHS) (AREA IN LAKHS HA.)

Category	*1980-81*			*1985-86*			*1990-91*		
	No.	*Area (hect)*	*Av.size*	*No.*	*Area (hect.)*	*Av.size*	*No.*	*Area (hect.)*	*Av. size*
Marginal Below 1.0 ha.	3.8	2.1	0.6	4.5	2.4	0.5	5.1	2.8	0.5
Small 1.0 ha-2.0 ha.	2.6	3.6	1.4	2.7	3.8	1.4	3.0	4.1	1.4
Semi-medium 2.0 ha-4.0 ha.	1.9	5.0	2.6	1.8	5.0	2.7	1.8	4.8	2.7
Medium 4.0 ha-10.0 ha	0.8	4.1	5.5	0.6	3.6	5.8	0.6	3.0	5.0
Large 10,0 ha and above.	0.1	0.9	13.2	0.05	0.7	14.4	0.03	0.5	16.7
All categories.	9.2	15.7	1.7	9.6	15.5	1.6	10.5	15.1	1.4

Compiled from source-Report on Number and Area of operational holding in Orissa 1990-91, Agricultural Census Commissioner, Orissa, pp. 23-24.

Tribal agriculture is characterised by declining farm size, increasing number of operational holding, higher degree of fragmentation and declining contribution of agriculture to their household economy, dependancy on minor forest produces (non-timber forest produces) restricted due to declinging forest area and species, as well as restriction of marketing of NTFP substantially reduced tribal economy, to subsistance economy.

THE DILEMMA OF TECHNOLOGICAL APPLICATION FOR ELIMINATING TRIBAL POVERTY AND BACKWARDNESS

There are several possibilites of contradicting desireable objectives with each other, always create a questionmark for successful eradicating tribal poverty. Higher productivity by application of high level of mechanisation may create a few rich in resources those who are educated and conscious but create unemployment and inequality, application of chemical pesticides may improve agricultural productivity through pest control but create environmental and health hazards when handled by illiterate Tribals by encouraging slash and burn cultivation (known as Swidden or shifting cultivation) may improve their nutrient level by increasing their food products but may cause soil erosion and loss of forest and so on.

Despite several continuous plans to develop tribals particularly the problem of poverty has remained more or less intact even though there has been a greater upsurge of science and technology. Unless right kind of technology has evolved and applied, the expenditure on Research and Development has been concentrated primarily in sectors of little relevance to poor forest levellers. Therefore one of the basic task is to build up a concensus on the nature of technologies relevant for eradication of Tribal poverty is to identify the conditions necessary for successful application after taking into account of factors affecting due to topography and climate, living style and culture, levels of skill education and social acceptability for them. To state it in other words, the appropriateness of a technology is basically a social issue, involving some questions relating to who gains and who loses and extent of such gains and loss need a clear cut guideline from social scientists and planners.

INDIAN PLANNING PROGRAMMES FOR ERADICATION OF RURAL POVERTY

The concept of growth with social justice is said to be basic to the philosophy of development underlying Indian economic planning. Since the first five year plan, it was acknowledged that "the rural population which constituted about 83 per cent of the total, suffers from chronic under employment and low incomes" (p.12). During last five decades embraced various programmes of land reforms, employment of agricultural and landless labour, irrigation projects, village and rural Industries rural financial and credit support, rural electrification, spread of literacy and training programme, *et al.* Evaluating the progress of rural development, the sixth five-year plan (1978-83) commented "in spite of massive investments made in the rural areas over the years, the pace and gains of development have remained disparate between areas, some of the areas continuing to lag behind. What is of even greater concern in this disparity is that a very large number of those who are economically weak and disadvantaged, still remain in absolute poverty zone. There has been, in fact, an increase in the number of such persons" (p. 303). After a review of special programmes of rural development, such as Small Farmers Development Agencies (SFDA), Marginal Farmers and Agricultural Labourers Development Agencies (MFAL). The area Development plans such as Draught Prone Area Programme (DPAP), Integrated Tribal Development Programmes (ITDP), Hill Area Development Programmes (HADP) Desert Development Programme (DDP), Command Area Development Programme (CADP), Intensive Agriculture District Programme (IADP), etc., are also unable to combat poverty.

The objective of developing the area through percolating its benefits to the people failed miserably as benefits concentrated in few households. Therefore, Mrs. Indira Gandhi started her campaign against poverty by creating a wave of slogans 'Garibi Hatao'. Accordingly during sixth plan special target groups were classified according to their possession of resources and socio economic conditions such as Small farmers, Marginal farmers, Agricultural labourers, rural artisans and as Scheduled Tribe, Scheduled Caste and Women.

The sixth plan proposed to attain within 10 years, (i) the removal of unemployment and significant under employment, (ii) appreciable rise in the standard of living of the poorest sections of the population and (iii) provision of some of the basic needs of the people in the low income groups like clean drinking water, elementary education, health care, adult literacy, rural roads and housing and minimum services. The sixth plan initiated Integrated Rural Development Programme and the earlier programme of SFDA and IMFAL merged with it with area development programmes.

The seventh plan document comment, after reviewing the acnievement of IRDP during sixth plan, that "Although there have been many shortcomings in the programme, there have been strong features also". During the sixth plan there was 10 per cent decline in the number of people below poverty line—from 48% in 1977-78 to 37.4% in 1983-84, the rural figures being from 51.2% in 1977-78 to 40.4% in 1983-84. The planners conclude that "There is now evidence to suggest that the process of economic growth and antipoverty programmes had made a significant dent in the problem of poverty" (Seventh plan, p. 32) and poverty programmes have to be viewed in the wider prospective of Socio-economic transformation in the country (Seventh plan, p. 50).

It is clear that to alleviate poverty by developing agriculture was the main motive of first few years planning in India, when land reform and irrigation development were given a pre-eminent place. Introducing new technology and increasing productivity per hectare and increasing crop intensity tilted its benefits towards prosperous farmers. The failure of agricultural growth to make a sizeable dent on rural poverty has led policy makers to focus attention on the strategy of 'direct attack on poverty through poverty alleviation programmes. Prof. Sen considered, "the political economy of targeting has to be concerned not just with the economic problems of selection, information and incentives but also with political support for, and feasibility of, aiming public policy specifically at removing deprivation of particular groups (Sen, 1995). Understanding how to alleviate poverty is a central concern of development economics. Although there is ample evidence that policies designed to foster economic growth significantly reduce poverty (Bruno, Squire, and Ravallion, 1995), policies aimed at alleviating poverty are also important.

TRIBAL SUB-PLAN

The total number of S.T. households in the State as per 1981 Census was 12.29 lakhs, 90% of these households were anticipated to have remained below the poverty line. Thus at the beginning of the sixth plan period 11.00 lakhs S.T. households were estimated to have been below poverty line of whom 4.98 lakhs were assisted under various anti poverty programmes during the sixth plan period, 6.02 lakhs S.T. families therefore remained to be assisted in the beginning of the 7th Plan.

One of the basic objective of the tribal sub-plan during the sixth plan was to maintain a balance between area development and the coverage of Scheduled Tribe beneficiaries under various poverty amelioration schemes. In other words coverage of tribal families will go on simultaneously with critical infrastructural development programmes so that the potential generated through the later can be utilised by the former in a best possible manner.

TABLE NO. 4.7

TARGET AND ACHIEVEMENT OF ANTI-POVERTY SCHEME FOR S.T.

Schemes	*Target for 6th Plan*	*Famlies economically assisted during the 6th plan period.*	*Percentage of achievement.*
I.R.D.	280654	219660	78.05
E.R.R.P	120000	102467	68.00
Spl. Central Assistance and other state plan schemes.	149346	175811	102.79
	550000	497938	90.00

Govt. of Orissa, Harijan and Tribal Welfare Dept. (1990) Annual Tribal Sub-plan, Orissa 1990-91 (Draft)

However, evaluation studies of 12 ITDAS shows that on an average 24% of the S.T. families assisted may have crossed the poverty lines by the end of the plan. It is presumed that 1.24 lakhs of S.T. families (25%) out of 4.98 lakhs, have been enabled to cross the poverty line during the sixth plan period and the remaining 3.74 lakhs S.T. families need supplementary dose of assistance to enable them to cross the poverty line during seventh plan period. (Tribal sub-plan 1990-91, p. 51).

The sub-plan strategy adopted for Tribal Development considered essentially an area development programme approach and this was streamlined during the sixth plan by launching a direct attack against poverty through individual family oriented income generating scheme.

The individual S.T. family is provided with 50 per cent subsidy of unit cost subject to a limit of Rs. 6,000/-. The rest 50 per cent of the scheme is borne under the assistance from the credit flow of the different credit institutions.

The programme wise proposed and actual coverage of families during eighth plan is as indicated in Table 4.8.

TABLE 4.8: TRIBAL FAMILIES PROPOSED AND COVERED DURING VIII PLAN PERIOD UNDER VARIOUS SCHEMES (1992-97)

Sl. No.	*Programes*	*Proposed*	*Families covered*	*Percentage of achievement.*
1.	2	3	4	5
1.	I.R.D.P.	221696	178572	80.55
2.	Assistance to Small and Marginal Farmers	7360	-	0.00
3.	I.T.D.A. Schemes	147500	204666	138.76
4.	MADA/Clusters	22000	20222	91.92
5.	Micro-projects	20000	6350	317.50
6.	S.C., ST, DFCC	25000	19804	79.22
7.	Sericulture	2500	--	0.00
8.	Fishery	2000	2959	147.95
9.	Million Well Scheme/ Soil conservations/ Horticulture/ Agriculture schemes.	10511	31325	298.02
		440567	463898	105.30

Source: Tribal Sub-plan for Ninth Plan 1997-2002 (pp. 86-87) and Annual Plan 1997-98.

JAWAHAR ROJGAR YOJANA (JRY)

JRY, a major wage employment programme was launched in the last year of the seventh plan by merging two ongoing wage employment programmes, viz., National Rural Employment Programme (NREP) and Rural Landless Employment Guarantee Programme (RLEGP). With Centre's share being 80 per cent and the states share 20 per cent implemented in all the villages in the country. Central assistance to the states for JRY is distributed in proportion to the rural poor of each state to the total number of rural poor in the country. But of this allocation for each state, 28 per cent is earmarked for various schemes at the state level (20 per cent earmarked for Million Well Schemes (MWS) for poor SC/ST farmers, 6 per cent for housing under the Indira Awas Yojana (IAY) and 2 per cent as administrative costs. The remaining 72 per cent is allocated to districts on the basis of an index of backwardness with 20 per cent weightage for the proportion of agricultural labourers in Total rural workers, 60 per cent weightage to the proportion of rural SC and ST population in relation to the total rural population and 20 per cent weightage to increase of agricultural productivity. Out of the district level allocations, 20 per cent is retained at the district level and 80 per cent is allocated to the village Panchayats by giving 60 per cent weightage to SC and ST population and 40 per cent to the total population of the village Panchayat. There is no sectoral earmarking at the village panchayat level except that 15 per cent of annual allocation directed to be spent on programmes (works) directly beneficial to SCs and STs and 30 per cent for women beneficiaries.

The Eighth Five Year Plan recognises that "there is a need for integrating the various anti-poverty programmes with the sectoral programmes in a specified area so as to ensure a sustainable increase in employment and income of the rural poor and the infrastructural and environmental development of the area" (Eighth five year plan, Vol. II, p. 37).

TABLE NO. 4.9: PERSON DAYS OF EMPLOYMENT GENERATED UNDER JRY IN ORISSA ACCORDING TO VARIOUS ETHNIC GROUPS. *Mandays in (Lakh Person Days)*

Year	*ST.*	*S.C.*	*O.C.*	*Total*
1989-90				517.63
1990-91	127.42	102.62	111.93	341.97
	(37.26)	(30.00)	(32.73)	(100.00)
1991-92	127.99	105.39	115.48	348.86
	(36.69)	(30.21)	(33.10)	(100.00)
1992-93	119.73	96.92	109.74	326.39
	(36.68)	(29.70)	(33.62)	(100.00)
1993-94	182.13	139.92	157.02	479.07
	(38.02)	(29.21)	(32.75)	(100.00)
1994-95	170.00	130.78	142.81	443.59
	(38.32)	(29.48)	(32.19)	(100.00)
	727.27	575.63	636.98	1939.88
	(37.49)	(29.67)	(32.36)	(100.00)
1996-97	115.09	96.65	102.45	314.19
	(36.68)	(30.76)	(32.61)	(100.00)

Source: Panchayat Raj Department, Government of Orissa, Bhubaneswar.

In the implementation of wage-employment programmes

priority is to be given to activities which improve the land resources base and eco-system in rural areas such as water harvesting, desilting of irrigation tanks, construction of field channels, drainage and measures for soil conservation including afforestation. These are best undertaken in the framework of watershed development in which micro watersheds are taken up for systematic treatment by using technologies that are area specific, cost effective, ecologically sound and locally acceptable.

According to Eighth Plan "Priority should be given to soil and water conservation, waste land development and social forestry followed by rural roads and rural housing (p. 37), all weather roads need to be given priority, particularly in tribal, hill and desert areas where inaccessibility to markets and to information and inputs is a severe bottleneck" (*ibid.*, p. 36) (Eighth five year plan, p. 36).

EMPLOYMENT ASSURANCE SCHEME (EAS)

EAS was introduced in the year 1993 with an objective to provide assured employment for 100 days to two labourers in each family who are in need and desirous of work but unable to find it. This programme covers in drought prone areas, desert areas, hill and tribal areas which are already covered under Revamped Public Distribution Systems.

TABLE NO. 4.10: PERSON DAYS OF EMPLOYMENS GENERATED UNDER EAS IN ORISSA BY ETHENIC GROUPS. *(Mandays in lakhs person days)*

EAS	*ST*	*SC*	*OC*	*Total*
1993-94	16.60	6.71	8.12	31.43
	(52.82)	(21.35)	(25.83)	(100.00)
1994-95	143.89	61.22	76.13	281.24
	(51.16)	(21.77)	(27.07)	(100.00)
1995-96	157.45	74.11	79.50	311.06
	(50.62)	(23.82)	(25.56)	(100.00)
1996-97	162.55	135.74	141.07	439.36
	(37.00)	(30.84)	(32.11)	(100.00)

Source: Panchayat Raj Department Government of Orissa, Bhubaneswar

The expenditure incurred under JRY in different years from 1990-91 to 1997 has been presented in Table 4.9. Table 4.9 shows that the share of employment days generated for ST is much higher than their other ethnic groups.

Person days of employment generated under EAS in Orissa during the period 1993-94 to 1996-97 has been discussed in Table 4.10. Table 4.10 depicts that the percentage of employment generated under EAS in Orissa for ST population is more than 50 per cent except the year 1996-97. However, in absolute terms, the person days of employment generated under EAS steadily increased.

The total number of beneficiaries including Scheduled Tribe beneficiaries and the amount of subsidy sanctioned under IRDP during the period 1980-81 to 1996-97 has been analysed in Table 4.11. Table 4.11 reveals that the percentage of beneficiaries differ from 17.81 in 1980-81 to 32.30 in 1990-91 in case of Scheduled Tribe population.

TABLE NO. 4.11: COVERAGE OF SCHEDULE TRIBES UNDER IRDP INTEGRATED RURAL DEVELOPMENT PROGRAMME

(Rs. in lakhs)

	Total beneficiaries	*of which S.T.*	*Subsidy on S.T.*	*Total subsidy*
1980-81	100,419	17,885 (17.81)	---	559.73
1981-82	138,367	30,724 (22.20)	283.80 (24.98)	1136.16
1982-83	252,453	54,822 (21.72)	577.61 (28.42)	2032.67
1983-84	217,073	59,394 (27.36)	641.01 (33.34)	1922.62
1984-85	213,119	56,835 (26.67)	605.87 (30.80)	1967.12
	832,431	219,660 (26.38)		
1985-86	173,427	44,522 (25.67)	585.52 (32.61)	1795.29
1986-87	207,872	53,320 (25.65)	656.43 (29.76)	2205.86
1987-88	221,726	56,090 (25.30)	833.91 (27.01)	3087.27
1988-89	223,462	71,536 (32.01)	910.89 (34.99)	2603.43
1989-90	188,788	56,646 (30.01)	838.67 (32.24)	2449.47
	1,015,275	282,114 (27.79)		
1990-91	149,612	48,327 (32.30)	1083.47 (35.19)	3078.62
1991-92	111,712	34,535 (30.91)	1063.74 (32.93)	3229.86
	261,324	82,862 (31.71)		
1992-93	93,226	28,838 (30.93)	950.45 (33.89)	2804.48
1993-94	172,899	50,246 (31.40)	1626.40 (31.44)	5173.57
1994-95	139.837	41,591 (29.74)		5221.79
1995-96	120.669	35,843 (29.70)		6048.92
1996-97	90,985	24,449 (26.87)		5808.87

Source: Economic Survey (1994-95, p-205) and P.R. Deptt. Govt. of Orissa.

During sixth plan, the number of beneficiaries of ST population was 26.38 per cent but during 7th plan 1985-86 to 1989-90 it was 27.79 per cent, which gradually picked up though it is marginal. But the share of subsidy in ST was more than their proportion. In other words, the percentage of beneficiaries is lower than the percentage of subsidy assured to ST population in Orissa.

Despite continuous and meaningful approach by Government to bring them to the mainstream of national economy, the tribals in Orissa still remained far away from expectation of our development planning.

REFERENCES

1. Bruno Michael, Lynsquire and Martin Ravallion (1995) 'Equity and growth in Developing Countries–Old and New Perspectives". Policy Research working paper 1563, World Bank, Washington D.C.

2. Galbraith, John Kenneth (N.A.) "Economic Development in Perspective, The United States Information Service.

3. UNESCO (1970). "Equality of Access of Women to Literacy" United Nations Educational and Cultural Organisation, p. 9.

4. Mangat, H.S. (1994). "World Bank Aid for Haryana" *The Tribune*, 1 October 1994, p. 94.

5. Government of Orissa, (1990). Annual Tribal Sub-Plan 1990-91. Harijan and Tribal Welfare Department.

6. Government of Orissa: (1996). Report on Number and Area of Operational Holdings in Orissa 1990-91. Agricultural Census Commissioner, Board of Revenue, Cuttack, Orissa.

7. Government of Orissa (1977). Tribal Sub-Plan for Ninth Plan 1997-2002 and Annual Plan 1997-98 Welfare Department, September, 1997, pp. 84-85

8. Sen, Amartya. (1995). "The Political Economy of Targeting" in Daminique Vander Walle and Kimberly Nead, Eds., Public Spending and the Poor, Theory and Evidence, Baltimore, Md. The John Hopkins University Press for the World Bank.

5

Tribal Economy–A Regional Study (A study in Phulbani District of Orissa)

Dr. S.N. Tripathy*

Next to Madhya Pradesh, the state of Orissa has the largest concentration of tribal population in India. There are 62 tribes in Orissa with a population of 6.99 lakhs (1991 census) which constitute about 22.2 per cent of the total population of the state.

TRIBALS OF ORISSA

The Tribal population of Orissa are concentrated in almost all the districts of the state. As per 1991 census the largest concentration of such people is in the district of Mayurbhanj where the tribal population is 57.8 per cent of the total population. The next in order of importance is the district of Koraput where the corresponding percentage is 54.3. The third place in this regard is occupied by Sundargarh with 50.7 per cent of tribal population. Keonjhar with 44.5 per cent of such people and Phulbani with 37.3 per cent of tribal population occupies fourth and fifth place respectively among the districts of Orissa. The tribes of Orissa have distinct features

* *Department of Economics, Aska Science College, Aska (Orissa) 761 111.*

and they fall into clearly definable anthropological groups. The Kolarian Tribes of Santals, Mundas and Hos occupy the northern districts of Mayurbhanj, Sundargarh and Sambalpur. The southern undivided districts of Koraput, Ganjam and Phulbani are inhabited by the principal tribes such as Khonds and Souras. The most primitive tribes of the country like Khonds, Savaras, Parajas, Koyas, Bottadas, Bonda Parjas, Gadabas, Gondos, Jatpurs, Matias, etc., are found in Orissa.[1]

HISTORICAL BACKGROUND

For centuries, the tribals have been living in the remote hills and forests, leading an independent life of their own. The Britishers came in contact with them in the beginning of the 19th century. They chose not to interfere with their economic lives. Administration in tribal areas, were kept separate from the normal administration of the general man. The policy of isolation was favourable to the non-tribals, viz., money-lenders, contractors, Zamindars and Middlemen to exploit them. In some areas the British rulers created "excluded" and "partially excluded" areas, allowed the tribals limited privileges and separate political representation.[2]

Imposition of heavy taxation, system of bethy and begari, stagnation of agriculture, exploitation of the peasants were the common socio-economic features during the British regime.[3]

The barriers posed by the mountains in the field of human mobility and transporation, lack of irrigation potential, scarcity of cultivable lands and extreme climatic conditions have all served to keep Khondmals isolated to a very great degree from the neighbouring plains of Orissa.[4]

However, like other segments, tribal society has been part of the universe of Indian civilization. Wide-ranging movements occurred against the colonial system which could be seen as part of the large anti-colonial struggle.[5] With slight variations the tribes have a highly egalitarian society, with high status for women, dignity of labour as a love of freedom as basic planks of their ethos. Despite centuries of onslaughts of external civilizations and modern influences some of them have been able to maintain their values as seen in their rites and rituals as also traditional institutions.

TRIBAL PROBLEMS OF PHULBANI

The district of Boudh-Khondamals known as Phulbani, covers 7.11 per cent of the total area of the state and ranks sixth among the districts in size. Concentration of tribal population is high in the district of Phulbani (39 per cent) as per 1981 census report. This figure is much higher than the state and national average of 22.43 per cent and 6.9 per cent respectively. The percentage of tribal populations falls by 3.8 per cent from 1951 to 1981 as revealed from Table 5.1. The tribal females of the district outnumbered the males. Twenty-seven types of tribes are numerically important, found in Phulbani. They are Gond Khond or Kondha or Sita Kandha, Mirdhas munda, Pentic, Saora or Savor or Saura, Suabar or Lodha.[7] The tribals of Phulbani depend on agricultural holdings, which are small, scattered and uneconomic. The income from such uneconomic holdings is meagre. As a result, they remain below the poverty line. 'Podu' cultivation is practised in hill slopes mostly by the tribals who constitute 41 per cent of the total population of the district.[8] Due to lack of sufficient arable lands and ploughing equipments the Kondh tribes are habituated in Podu cultivation. This is considered as a laborious, dangerous and wasteful procedure of cultivation. The forest areas of the district are increasingly declining because of 'Podu' cultivation, large-scale deforestation. The total forest area of the district to the total geographical area was 82 per cent by 1975-76 and by 1980-81 it was reduced to 53 per cent.

TABLE : 5.1: SCHEDULED TRIBE POPULATION OF THE DISTRICT PHULBANI

(*Figures in 1000*)

Census Year.	*Scheduled Tribe (ST)*			*% of ST population to the total population*
	Male	*Female*	*Total*	
1951	97.3	97.9	195.2	42.7
1961	104.3	109.8	214.1	41.6
1971	122.8	127.8	250.6	40.3
1981	137.0	142.3	179.6	38.9

Source : Figures compiled from:

(i) Statistical Hand Book, Phulbani 1964. 65, p. 9.

(ii) Statistical Abstract, Government of Orissa, 1971, pp. 30-31.

(iii) Provisional figures of 1981 census report.

The low proportion of irrigation, erratic distribution of rainfall, high periodicity of droughts and unfertile nature of the soil are the significant factors responsible for the backwardness of the district. Collection of minor forest produce is an important source of livelihood for the tribals.

A perusal of the study brings into light that decline in forest area due to 'Podu' or Shifting cultivation', restriction imposed by the government on the use of the forest by the tribal people, decline in the agricultural productivity, large-scale transfer of land to the non-tribals, uncertain rainfalls, frequent crop failures—all these entangle the tribals in the web of poverty and misery.

GOVERNMENT POLICY

Protection of tribals from exploitation and their socio-economic development have received attention of the government, after independence. Special safe-guards were incorporated in the constitution of India and various problems of tribals came to the fore-front. Article 46 of the constitution has clearly laid down that "the state shall promote the special case of the educational and economic interests of the weaker sections of the people and in particular of Scheduled Castes and Scheduled Tribes, and shall protect them from social injustice and all forms of exploitation". Similarly, suitable provisions have also been made under the fifth and sixth Schedules of the constitution, particularly with reference to the protection of tribal land, allotment of waste land and protection from exploitation by money-lenders. The Orissa Transfer of Immovable Property (by Scheduled Tribes) Resolution, 1956 provides for the control and check of the transfer made by the Scheduled Tribes to the non-Scheduled Tribes in scheduled areas. The Bonded Labour System (Abolition) Act, 1976 provides for the abolition of bonded labour system (Gothi) with a view to preventing the economic and physical exploitation of the weaker sections of the people.

Commendable efforts have been made during the plan periods for tribal development . One of the important problems of development in tribal areas is how best to reconcile the objectives of bringing about desired socio-economic transformation and preserving their cultural autonomy. There has been increasing emphasis on ameliorating their economic condition, break the isolation of the tribal society and integrate them into the national mainstream.

TRIBAL SUB-PLAN

Area having more than 50 per cent tribal concentration has been selected for the implementation of Integrated Tribal Development Agency (ITDA) which serves as the unit of planning and executes development programmes. The tribal sub-plan aims at comprehensive development with focus on the individual family. The families living below the poverty line are identified, their needs and problems are reviewed, and appropriate programmes are executed. Apart from core economic sectors like agriculture, animal husbandry, horticulture, etc., sufficient emphasis was laid on education. In tribal areas infrastructure was poorly developed and therefore, capacity for the absorption of funds was very low. This problem is now mitigated by quantified investment in the tribal areas for infrastructure and individual family development.

There are two Integrated Tribal Development Agencies functioning in Phulbani in the Sub-Plan area. Balliguda I.T.D.A. covers 9 blocks of Balliguda Sub-Division and Phulbani I.T.D.A covers 3 blocks of Khondamals Sub-Division. The main thrust of I.T.D.P., as noted earlier, is two fold, i.e., development of initial infrastructure like communication, education, mini-irrigation and plantation and income generation of tribal families living below the poverty line.

A sum of Rs. 46.89 lakhs has been utilised by Balliguda I.T.D.A. and Rs. 23.95 lakhs by Phulbani I.T.D.A. in development of infrastructure. The amount has been spent on development of agriculture, in tribal welfare education institutions, supply of teaching aids to such schools, low cost hostels, plantation of minor forest produce, etc. The year wise expenditure during the sixth plan period is indicated in Table 5.2.

TABLE: 5.2

Year	*Balliguda ITDA*	*Phulbani ITDA*
1980-81	7.45	3.95
1981-82	9.97	5.27
1982-83	3.65	5.86
1983-84	10.71	2.62
1984-85	15.11	6.25
Total	46.89	23.95

Source : District Rural Development Agency Office, Phulbani.

In the state of Orissa there are 31.87 per cent of the total tribal population which are scattered in some areas and found in lesser concentration in other areas outside the Tribal sub-plan. Such tribal pockets are known as Modified Area Development Pocket (M.A.D.A) for the dispersed tribals living in five Grampanchayats of Boudh Block of Phulbani District, M.A.D. A. Scheme is in operation since 1978.

KUTIA KHOND DEVELOPMENT AGENCY (K.K.D.A)

Kutia Khond is a primitive tribe living in the top of Belghar hill situated at a height of more than, 2,000 feet above the sea level in Phulbani District. For their development a Micro Project, namely, 'Kutia Khond Development Agency' has been established in 1978.

Apart from the developmental schemes analysed above, some other development programmes like Drought-Prone area Programme (D.P.A.P.), District Rural Development Agency (D.R.D.A) and Fish Farmer's Development Agency (F.F.D.A.) are in vogue for alleviation of poverty and to bring about a change in socio-economic life of the tribals. But so for, these agencies have not produced any visible transformation in socio-economic life of the tribals of Phulbani.

Despite developmental plans, spread of financial institutions, and other measures, it has been observed that the tribals are exploited by Mahajans and businessmen. The distressed sale of agricultural produce and forest collections by tribals to the Mahajans and businessmen have resulted in poor economic conditions of tribals.[9]

Therefore, it is highly imperative to develop the skill, knowledge and awareness among the tribal people coupled with income generating labour-intensive schemes in tribal areas through the development of agriculture, infrastructure, horticulture, etc.—which can bring about a catalystic change in their socio-economic conditions.

REFERENCES

1. Annual Administrative Reports of Scheduled Castes and Scheduled Tribes, 1960-61. Tribal and Rural Welfare Department, Government of Orissa, pp. 2-3.

2. Vidyarthi, L.P. and Rai, B.K., "The Tribal Culture of India" (1977) pp. 412-14.

3. Tripathy, S.N. (Dr). *Bonded Labour in India,* Discovery Publishing House, New Delhi (1989), p. 80.

4. Bailey, F.G. "Caste and Economic Frontier" (A Village in High Land of Orissa). Oxford University Press, 1962, p. 245.

5. Singh, S.K. "*Tribal Society in India*, Manohar Publications, New Delhi (1985), p.18.

6. Nayak, R.K. (Dr.). Tribal World in Orissa in a state of Flux, Social Welfare, April 1990, p. 25.

7. Census of India, 1960, Orissa District Census Hand-book, Boudh-Khondamals pp. 15-16.

8. Annual Administrative Report 1980-81 and 1981-82. District Rural Development Agency (D.R.D.A.), Phulbani, p. 15.

9. Tripathy, S.N. *Bonded Labour in India. op. cit.*

6

Tribal Development and Institutional Finance in Koraput Region (Orissa)

Dr. Eswar Rao Patnaik*

There are more than 70.34 lakhs tribal population in the economy of Orissa. On the other hand, there are 427 Scheduled Tribes in India. Prior to independence, some leeway in tribal Development was made, thanks to Christian missionaries and Thakkar Bappa. The British rulers, by and large followed a "leave them alone policy".

It must be noted that, the right to life does not only mean the right to bare animal level of subsistence: it really means the right to live with human dignity. With the advent of planning in India, the policy for tribes have taken positive turns in inaugurating an era of socio-economic development for the tribal areas and tribal people. Tribal development blocks were created. It is possible to think of five levels of deprivation of tribals, viz.: (1) Non-recognition of rights over resources and restrictions on their use, (2) alienation of worker from the means of production, (3) denial of due entitlement of labour, (4) barter of personal liberty, (5) the psychological states of deprivation as justified.

* *Dr. Patnaik, Reader in Economics, Government College, Bhawanipatna, Kalahandi Dt. (Orissa)*

Development has created an urge among tribesmen to emulate caste Hindu standards in relation to birth, marriage and death. So, today, the extent of indebtedness among the tribals has increased manifold. The marginal size of land holding, the slender irrigation base of the economy and addiction to the wine drags the "Adivasi" to the whirlphool of indebtedness.

Money-lenders and land-lords were the premier sources of finance in rural areas, prior to nationalisation of the commercial banks. The method of borrowing from land-lords and money-lenders was found to be costly and exploitative. The failure of indebted families to redeem the loans of shy-lock like money-lender has led to the pitiable situation of dispossession of lands owned by tribals. So, plan endeavour at country level has embarked on Multi-Agency Approach to credit, with cooperative societies, commercial banks and R.R.Bs, as the partners in development. The approach was directed to

(i) Secure an increase in the volume of institutional credit;

(ii) Serve the economically weaker section of society;

(iii) reduce regional imbalances in the pace of development and flow of credit.

OBJECT OF THE PAPER

The object of the present paper is to analyse and assess the performance of banks and cooperatives in Koraput district. It seeks to answer the question: Have the Banks succeeded in serving the economically weaker section of society? The study may provide us theoretical insights into credit and related activities of tribals of a region. The study may also be useful for policy making purposes.

II

REVIEW OF LITERATURE

There is a large and learned literature on tribal development. In "Tribal Agriculture in India" (1979), the author (Samal Jagabandhu) has pointed out that, the land operated by the tribals was of poor quality and presumably for this reason, the tribals were considered risky to finance by banks. The marginal size of land holdings along with the subsistence nature of agricultural operations deters them from making long-term development in agriculture. He concludes that, the procedures and formalities followed by cooperatives in their lending activities make them unsuitable, as sources of finance for agriculture.

The present paper draws strength from "The tribal problems of today and tomorrow" (1978) edited by P.C. Mohapatro and D. Panda, Sabari Cultural Society, Bhubaneswar. The work is a collection of write-ups of eminent scholars of different shades. "Problems of Tribal Economy of Orissa" by Dr. Baidyanath Mishra, pleads for integrating credit with market link to enable the hills-man to secure fair return for his produce. He appeals to voluntary organisations to organise Socio-economic activities of tribals, so that, they are assured of food, fodder, fuel, fruits and fair return.

"Some thoughts on tribal development" by B.D. Sharma reasons that, money-lending by private individuals should not remain worthwhile, through induction of alternative supply lines. He suggests that, the pre-existing debts of tribals should be cancelled in one stroke and contact points between tribals and outsiders are not to be of a economic nature.

Provision of interest free loans without any security, scaling down of debts and creation of economically advantageous occupations for the low income group were the lines of advance advocated by Gopinath Mohanty for Tribal Development in his paper "New Horizons and Old".

"The Strategy of Development of Tribal Economy of Orissa with a reference to Koraput District" by Dr. P.C. Mohapatra quotes that, tribal families are born in debt, live in debt and die in debt. The imprudent nature of tribals to spend lavishly on ceremonies like "Chaitro Parba" and other rituals compels them to borrow money from shahukars. He refers to the psychological state of debtor, when he adds that, "For some at least all happiness is lost". He concludes that, a system of bonded labour is the by-product of indebtedness among tribal families.

The editor of the Tribals in India, the changing scenario, Dr. S.N. Tripathy mentions that, any disease or suffering in a tribal family leads to loans from a crafty money-lender, who is always watchful of adivasi's needs. The silver linings in the clouds are cooperatives and banks.

III

STATEMENT OF THE PROBLEM

It has been hypothesised that, of late banks have made rapid strides in serving agriculture and rural development. Nevertheless, traders and money-lenders, till today dominate the rural scene for supply of credit.

METHOD OF STUDY

The present study is based on field work and desk work. The findings of the study are based on a survey of the three blocks in the undivided Koraput region, i.e., Narayana Patna, Kotpad and Jeypore blocks in 1987-88. With a view to assessing the extent of progress achieved by the economy in credit sphere, a study of Koraput district carried out by Dr. P.C. Mohapatro in 1977-78 was taken into consideration.

The academic exercise is based on simple multi stage Random sampling technique. The study has covered 389 households spread in seventeen villages of the district. For tabulation work, simple arithmetic average was used. Developments pertaining to one year may not hold good for all persons, at all places. Lapse of memory on the part of respondent households is possible.

IV

CHARACTERISTICS OF THE AREA AND PEOPLE

The ratio of Scheduled Caste and Scheduled Tribe population in sample villages is 24.165% and 58.169% respectively. The ratio of Scheduled Caste and Scheduled Tribe population at district level, on the other hand, is 14.6% and 55.29% respectively. The study area is inhabited by tribes like, Kondhs, Koyas, Jatapu and Saoras. The literacy accomplishment of the people of the region is 28%.

It is well known that, the tribals operate at a low level of economic activity and have low accessibility to modern technology and marketing facility. Being fatalistic by nature, they believe that, they can not change their destiny. They lead a communal life and live in harmony with nature. There is no written script for their languages. They have low cognitive skill, present time orientation and a kind of impulsiveness in which future does not figure.

The average size of population per sampled household is 5.98. The average size of land holding is 5.34 acres. But, 66% of cultivators are marginal and small farmers. Landlessness characterises 17% of households. Merely 9.34% of total cultivated land is covered by irrigation facilities. Agriculture provides sustenance for 83.6% of people of the area. The progress achieved in road development of the district appears to be something like finger tips on the iceberg, when we note that, the poverty-ridden economy of Koraput region has merely 43 km roads per square kilometre and these are not surfaced roads. Plan endeavour has succeeded in electrifying only 40.7% of villages of the district.

Out of 389 surveyed households, 90 families were steeped in debt. The average size of loan which was Rs. 367 in 1977-78 has picked up to Rs. 1727.83 in the district in 1987-88.

The possible reasons for the quantum increase in the size of loan of indebted household might be the uneconomic size of land holding, cultivation with crude techniques of cultivation, the presence of dry lands in the district and transfer of lands from tribal farmers to non-tribals due to non-recovery of loans. It is possible that, the imprudent nature of tribes-men to spend lavishly on feasts and ceremonies like "Chaitro Parbo" has intensified the grip of indebtedness among tribals.

V

The district's, economy is served by 250 commercial bank branches and 236 cooperative societies. Plan endeavour was directed to convert cooperatives into LAMPS, in line with the suggestions of

Bhave Committee. It is premature to draw a dividing line between credit transactions in cash and credit transactions in kind, because, field studies have confirmed that, indebted families have resorted to loans partly in cash and partly in kind.

ALLOCATION OF CREDIT IN THE AREA—SOURCE WISE

A perusal of Table 6.1 reveals that, commercial banks, co-operatives and Rural banks assume the order of priority in disbursement of credit among indebted families. The government does not figure in rural finance in 1977-78 as well as in 1987-88 probably, because, like a shock absorber, government provides loans to people only in periods of distress. Money-lender (Shahukars) and traders deserve attention among the non-institutional sources of finance.

The relative share of financing agriculture by non-institutional sources of finance has sharply declined from 22.58% in 1977-78 to 12.98% in the district. It follows that, there has been an increase in the relative share of institutional finance for agriculture from 77.42% in 1977-78 to 87.12% in 1987-88 in the district. In the province of Orissa also, the relative share of Banks in financing agriculture has picked up from 4.1% in 1951-52 to 10.76% in 1961-62, till it has reached 42% in 1980-81. It is possible, that, the multi-agency approach to credit has succeeded in its mission of securing an increase in the volume of institutional credit for agriculture.

It is heartening to note that, commercial banks are making credit available to farm population of the area partly in cash and partly in form of dusters and sprayers. Efforts were made by banks to expand branches in the district and to provide consultancy services to farmers of the area, through a team of agriculture experts, owned by the department.

Even a cursory glance at Table 6.1, makes it clear that, the relative share of cooperative societies in financing agriculture has picked up from the paultry percentage of 4.4% (of total credit) in 1977 to an impressive level of 30.479% in 1987 in the district. The finding is corroborated by developments in province of Orissa, where the share of cooperatives in rural finance has shot up from 2.7% (of total credit) in 1951 to 6.57% in 1961-62 and eventually, it stood at 38% in 1981-82.

6.1: VOLUME AND PERCENTAGE OF CREDIT BORROWED FROM DIFFERENT SOURCES BY SAMPLED HOUSEHOLDS IN STUDY AREAS OF KORAPUT DISTRICT (1987-88)

		Volume and Percentage of Loans Borrowed in Rupees						
Sources of Borrowing	*No.of House Holds*	*Narayan-Patna Block.*	*No of House Holds*	*Jeypore Block*	*No. of House Holds*	*Kotpad Block*	*Total No. of House Holds*	*Total amount of Loan.*
(1)	(2)	(3)	(4)	(5)	(6)	(7)	(8)	(9)
State Bank of India	07	20,300 (22.718 %)	04	13,000 (8.491 %)	09	1,10,471 (49.304 %)	20	1,43,771 (30.315) %)
Cooperatives	04	20,190 (22.595 %)	07	59,801 (39.059 %)	08	62,200 (27.760 %)	19	1,42,191 (30.479 %)
Rural Banks	11	33,265 (37.227 %)	09	60,300 (39.385 %)	05	26,687 (11.910 %)	25	1,20,252 (25.776 %)
Money Lenders	03	13,300.47 (14.884 %)	04	12,000 (7.837%)	06	13,500 (8.256 %)	13	43,800.47 (9.3881 %)
Land lords	Nil	Nil	03	7,000 (4.572 %)	03	5,600 (2.499 %)	06	12,600 (2.70 %)
Relatives	03	2,300 (2.574 %)	02	1,000 (0.653 %)	02	600 (0.267 %)	07	3,900 (0.835 %)
Total	28	89,355.47	29	1,53,101	33	2,24,658	90	4,66,514,47 (100 %)

Average size of loan per household from 1985 to 1987= 5,183.49 or 5,183.50
Annual Credit requisite of a cultivating house hold = Rs. 1,727.83.
Sources : (1) B. Eswar Rao Patnaik & Mohapatra, P.C. : Toning up Agriculture in Kotpad Block, Orissa Economic Journal, 1989, Vol. XXII, No. 1 & 2, p. 72.
(2) Sample Survey, 1987-88.

It appears that, only cooperatives can teach the farmers to borrow at right time in right quantity, for right purpose. One flower in their garland of successes is the personal touch they provide to the farmers. Rural minded credit can be evolved in village areas, only by cooperative socities, through motivation of people for activities, like parsimony and productive use of loans.

More than 72 per cent of total credit needs of indebted households flowed from R.R.Bs in 1977-78 in the district. However, in 1987, the R.R.Bs could finance credit needs of population to the extent of 25.7 per cent only. The observed trend may be due to low level of business of banks, want of lucrative salary of Bank employees, and operational problems pertaining to want of pucca houses to locate branches and access roads in villages. These difficulties are compounded by mounting overdues. It is an irony that, the sponsoring commercial banks do not depute senior officials but depute Junior officials having no training in non-power management in Gramin Banks, in keeping with their low cost philosophy.

Among the non-institutional sources of finance money-lenders/land lords, traders and relatives deserve attention. It was flashed by the Koraput survey of P.C. Mohapatro, 1977 that 21.20% of total credit of farm population of the region has flowed from money-lenders. In the concurrent survey of 1987, however, merely 9.38% of total borrowings of farm population of study areas flowed from money-lenders. The emerging scene at national level also indicates that, money-lender's role in rural finance is under eclipse, revealing a sharp decline from 70% in 1950-51 to 67.4% in 1960-61 and finally it stood at 13.8% in 1980-81.

The convincing explanations for the underlying tendency are the exorbitantly high rates of interest charged by them (as high as 50%), the non-issue of receipts for loans redeemed and compulsions on the debtor to sell produce to the creditor at unremunerative prices. The money lender's lending to farmers was largely in form of Paddy.

A new dimension of the enquiry is that, the less developed the economy is, the greater is the role of money-lender in rural finance. Thus, in the less developed block of Narayanapatna, 14.884% of total credit of farm population flowed from money-lenders, while the corresponding average in relatively more developed regions of Kotpad and Jeypore blocks were 8.256% and 7.837% respectively.

The reluctance of the cooperative societies to lend money for consumption purposes, create a credit gap for tribals for the fulfilment of which, they turn to money-lenders, who readily comply. As underscored by the Report of the Scheduled Areas and Scheduled Commission, 1960-61 "The money-lender is near at hand in the tribal village, speaks his own dialectic and knows the entire family history and the circumstances leading to debtor's need of money. It is deplorable to discern that, the debtor returns double the amount of produce he has borrowed from the creditor. The money-lender has nothing to commend it, except ready availability and flexibility.

Reference may be made of traders, who lend to farmers in form of cash, charge high rates of interest and cause under pricing for farm produce in the village.

So, we have tested the hypothesis: of late Banks have made rapid strides in serving agriculture and rural development. Nevertheless, traders and money-lenders, till today dominate the rural scene for supply of credit.

Records reveal that, the amount of loan incurred by a sampled household tended to increase with the size of landholding and it tended to decline with a decrease in the size of holding. It follows that, our credit system is more security oriented than need based.

The daunting task of agricultural planners is to transform static credit into dynamic credit. Credit is deemed static, when after paying interest and recovery of debt, the assets of the farmer and his capacity to produce and maintain levels of consumption for himself and his family remains unchanged.

The studies give rise to the following suggestions, which may be considered for policy making.

(1) Abolition of Bonded Labour

Indebtedness has set in motion a train of evils, like, usury and bonded labour. Bonded labour, which is locally known as "Kambari system" had its roots in Jeypore region. A "Goti", is a person, who after receiving some money in cash or kind engages himself by a written or oral agreement to labour under his creditor for agriculture and domestic purposes, as long as loan together with interest remains unpaid. It seems that, consumption loans are incurred by poorer classes of tribals living below subsistence level offering marginal security. The higher rate of interest charged compels them to part with their assets pushing them to a state of poverty.

The 20 point programme announced by the Prime Minister on July, 1st, 1975 is the first target oriented programme, to alleviate poverty in the country. The Orissa Money-lenders Act, 1939, the Orissa Money-lenders Regulation 1949, the Money-lenders Regulation 1967, and the Bonded Labour System Abolition Act were the notable steps taken up by State Government of Orissa to put an end to socio-economic exploitation in the country.

1. Against the back drop of 28.15% level of literacy of people in study area, it would be an over estimate to expect them to be conversant with the lending procedures and programmes of institutional agencies of credit. Hence, Banks may enlighten the people of the ongoing programmes, apart from quick disposal of borrower's credit files, considering the fact that, the olympian success of Danish Cooperative Society is in no small measure due to high literacy level of its members.

2. It has been officially estimated that the per capita deposit in the district is Rs. 253 and per capita advance is Rs. 254. These trends are deplorable and pin point the need for accelerating the pace of savings in the economy, through inculcating proper parsimony and motivation in minds of rural folk by Banks.

3. One more gap in the working of the credit system of the economy is, the lack of provision for supportive services for customers like, marketing facilities by Banks. In this context, it may be pointed out that, the system of integrating credit with marketing, which was tried first in sales in 30's with success was recommended by the Government of India in cooperative sector. Banks may venture in marketing lines,

so that, the share going to the farmer would increase and so also his ability to save. So credit should never be allowed to operate in vaccum.

4. One more operational problem confronting Banks in study area is the heavy load of overdues, that undermine their strength. For study area as a whole, the overdues of all institutional agencies of credit is rated at 53.55% in 1987-88, as against the National average of 58%. Available statistics, suggest that overdues position is the least in Maryanpatna block, i.e., 43.06 % and highest at Kotpad block, i.e., 62.49%, while the corresponding figure is 45.95% for Jeypore block. The prevalence of staggeringly high overdues is not conducive for the economy, as, N.A.B.A.R.D. has already declared its intent of forfeit of refinancing for State Governments which do not abide by its directives.

So, to improve the recovery performance of Banks: (1) Sufficient field staff may be provided for Banks, because Banks in study area are understaffed and 30% causes of non-recovery was accounted for by this factor. (2) One welcome suggestion for improving the recovery, drive is to avoid financing of non-feasible projects like, dug wells. (3) Mode of payment to borrowers may be in kind against borrowers acknowledgement of material receipts.(4) The period or redemption of loan may be carefully drawn, so that, the borrower is called for recovery of loans at a time, when he is in possession of funds. 20% of non-recovery cases stems from lacunae in the sphere. (5) Numerous studies on Indian Agriculture rightly advocate that the sponsoring agencies should share the responsibility for recovery of loans through extension services. (6) As suggested by the Kamath working group credit should he utilised for approved purposes only.

Further, genuine default due to inclemental weather like floods may be looked with sympathy through re-scheduling of loans, while wilful default due to callous indifference of the debtor partly may be subject to severe penalty.

5. One of the structural defects of the existing Banking system is inadequate growth of Banks in study areas, both in geographical and functional coverage. As yet, Banks have not penetrated into remote areas, like Bhaliaput villages in

Narayanpatna Block, while in Jeypore Block villages are well served by Banks. Thus islands of poverty have grown in the ocean of prosperity. Our stand point is corroborated by similar views, credit gaps have been noted in several sectors of the economy. The principles and policies of Banks are to be so formulated, that can effectively subserve backward areas and achieve the twin objectives of optimum growth with social justice.

TABLE: 6.2. OVER DUE POSITION OF BANKS IN STUDY AREA 1987-88.

Name of the Block.	*Name of the Bank*	*Amount of Credit (Rs.)*	*Amount of recovery in Rs./%.*	*Amount of over due in Rs./%*
Narayanpatna	B.B.I	20,300.00	7,714.00 (38%)	12,586.00 (62%)
	K.P.C.B.	33,265.00	20,757.36 (62.4%)	12,507.64 (37.6%)
	LAMPS	20,190.00	13,527.30 (67 %)	6,662.76 (33 %)
Total		73,755.00	41,998.66 (56.94 %)	31,756.34 (43.06 %)
Kotpad	S.B.I	1,10,471.00	24,303.62 (22 %)	86,167.38 (78 %)
	K.P.C.B.	26,687.00	10,541.36 (39.5%)	16,145.64 (60.5%)
	LAMPS	62,200.00	39,932.40 (64.2%)	22,267.60 (35.8%)
Total		1,99,358.00	74,777.38 (37.51%)	1,24,580.62 (69.49 %)
Jaypere	S.B.I.	13,000.00	3,510.00 (27%)	9,490.00 (73 %)
	K.P.C.B.	60,300.00	29,064.60 (48.2%)	31,235.40 (51.88%)
	LAMPS	59,801.00	39,349.06 (65.8%)	20,451.94 (34.2 %)
Total		1,33,101.00	71,923.66 (54.04 %)	61,177.34 (45.96 %)
Grand Total		4,06,214.00	1,88,699.7 (46.45 %)	2,17,514.3 (53.53 %)

Source : Sample Survey, 1987-88.

6. One problem area for the Banks is to how to secure scrupulous use of funds. It is a matter of grave concern that, there has been embezzlement of funds by an official in L.A.M.Ps. in Narayanpatna Block. Notwithstanding the penalty taken against the guilty party, the cultivators are fear-stricken and fight shy of approaching cooperative Banks. So, to strengthen the role of a cooperative society, as a vehicle of development, it is imperative that Bank employees should be imbibed with a high sense of duty and morality. Defective audit and control may inhibit the functioning of Banks and hence sound audit principles may be followed.

7. Attention may be paid to marginal and small farmers, who comprise roughly 37.542 % and 19.886 % of total farmers respectively in study areas. They are at the lowest rung of the ladder in respect of credit allotment, because nobody wants to be a guarantor for the poor debtor. The Bank's demand material security for provision of credit and the poor lack it. So, to obviate the difficulty, Banks may sanction greater amount of funds to the poor, after motivating them in self-employment schemes. Experience shows that, it is advantageous to set up a committee, consisting of people's representatives, Bank officials and poor farmers to consider the viability of the scheme. A sensible approach seems, that credit can be more effective, if Banks ensure forward and backward linkages, such as opening up of a beneficiary shop at Bank level, so that, the Bank may ensure fair prices for the agricultural produce of poor farmers.

8. There is a body of opinion that believes that reluctance of Banks to provide consumption based credit is a constraint in the working of Banks. It is probably for this reason, that money lender has played a greater role in backward block of Narayanpatna, than in developed Kotpad block. One scholar observes wisely "what was important for the marginal existence of the marginal farmer was consumption credit". So the

provision of consumption oriented credit by banks, may minimise the frequency of borrowings from exploitative money lenders.

9. It would be the 8th wonder of the world that, Rural Banks are making feeble efforts for combining low cost philosophy with efficiency in management at district and state levels. The genuine demands of ensuring betterment of rural areas through credit, calls for deputation of senior officials exposed to work in rural areas at branch level, even though the salary of senior officials has to be lucrative. In addition, the official of all cadres need training in man-power management and supervision of credit. Instead of appointing junior officials at Branch level senior officials may be deputed.

10. Experience shows that, credit may not be harnessed in productive channels in the low income economy of Koraput, in view of the tremendous amount of intoxication habits of farmers, which claims as high as 30% of their outlay. An authority on Koraput district, touches upon this aspect of tribals "the most primitive tribes are the worst addicts". So, voluntary agencies may refrain the public from intoxication tendencies, through informal education and persuasion.

11. The survey of 1987, highlights the crying need for appointing more field staff for serving the rural folk and for expediting the recovery of loans.

12. As yet, supervision of use of credit has not been tried seriously in the economy. The system of supervised credit refers to an endeavour of credit supplying agencies, that aims at improving both production and family living by coordinating credit provision with extension services. It has been tried in Latin America, with a measure of success, and includes preparation of farm production and home plan, and contemplates to assist poor farmers, who are potentially worthy to be credit worthy. So, Banks may be manned with Agriculture experts, who can educate enthusiastic farmers, on

technological aspects of production and hence the crop yield may be high.

13. The Government of Orissa has no doubt introduced crop loan insurance measures in the economy right, from the inception of the 6th 5 year plan, as a safety value against distress periods like flood, during which damage will be partly borne by the insuring company. The workability of the scheme was defunct as Ragi is not covered by the scheme.

14. One missing link in the working of credit agencies in study area is the absence of proper coordination between credit and non-credit activities, which follow production, i.e., storage, processing and marketing. This can be well illustrated by the fact that tobacco growers of Narayanpatna Block are engaged in distress sales of tobacco to itinerant traders at 970 rupees for a quintal, i.e., Rs. 30/- less than price prevailing at block level as processing facillties for tobacco are not available by organised agency and storage. This indicates the need for provision of storage and processing facilities by extension agencies for affecting improvement in productivity and repaying capacity of the peasant.

15. In fine, there is an urgent need for effective implementation of Money Lenders Act 1939, the Orissa Money Lenders Regulation Act and Debt Relief Acts of 1975, so as to counterweigh the malpractices of shylock-like money lender. Conventional wisdom may caution the welfare Government to exercise restraint before promulgamation of loan waiving programmes to the tune of Rs. 10,000/- per family, as it may cripple the financial soundness of Banks and render the farmer unscrupulous.

SUMMARY AND CONCLUSION

Development has to accord priority to low income group and small and marginal farmers. Development has to ensure and enhance people's entitlements. Strategies of development should enhance people's share in raising national income. Then only it becomes possible to arouse people's aspirations and motivation for higher living standards. The philosophy of development teaches us to emphasise values, like, love, freedom, confidence, self esteem and humanism.

An analysis of the progress of Banks and cooperatives has shown that, over a period of time, there has been an impressive increase in the relative share of institutional sources of finance for agriculture in Koraput region. The likely reasons for the observed trend may be usurious and exploitative nature of money-lenders and initiation of various regulatory measures by State Government on lending practices of money-lenders and traders. Some thrust are as for Banks, however, are penetrations into geographically isolated villages, like, Bhaliaput and dryland agriculture. Agricultural credit is a part of an integrated process of economic development and social betterment, provided credit is supplemented by complementary measures, like extension services and tenurial reforms.

The World Development Report pertinently counsels the Banker that, credit is an effective instrument for bringing about income transfers to the poor. To what extent, Banks will take cognisance of their current security based approach to credit allotment and contemplate on need based approach to credit, is a moot point. That requires the Banks and extension agencies to make orchestral endeavour to identify potential enterprises, tap their latent skills, train them in farming enterprise and motivate them on productive uses of credit in study areas. The formidable task can be accomplished, only if responsible Bank employees, sympathetic and sensitive public authorities and enthusiastically responsive public move together to fulfil the mission of the service approach of Banks, adopted by the Reserve Bank of India by the Act of 1989. The field staff of Banks may have to give up their present attitude to dwell in comfortable urban areas and penetrate into remote rural areas for serving the rural masses. Herein lies the secret of transforming a subsistence economy into a dynamic economy with an accent on Rural minded credit. The Banks should underscore the fact that the main objective of public credit system should be to benefit more and more small and marginal farmers and for reducing disparities.

TABLE 6.3: THE PERCENTAGE SHARE OF DIFFERENT SOURCES OF RURAL CREDIT IN ORISSA.

Sources	*Year (Percentage) 1951-52*	*Year (Percentage) 1961-62*	*Year (Percentage) 1971-72*	*Year Percentage 1979-80*
1. Institutional	4.1%	10.76%	N.A.	42%
(a) Government	1.4%	4.19%	N.A.	Nil
(b) Cooperatives	2.7%	6.57%	11.1%	38%
(c) Commercial Banks.	Nil	Nil	*N.A.	4%
2. Non-Institutional sources.	95.9%	89.24%	81.6%	58%

Source : Patro, N.P., Financing Agriculture by the State Cooperative Bank in Orissa, 1984 Thesis (pp. 100-102).

* The total percentage of loan provided by different sources to indebted families must necessarily be equal to 100, though the share of loan offered by commercial banks to borrowers was not available in Orissa State in 1971-72.

NOTES AND SELECTED REFERENCES

1. B.N. Das, "Appraisal and Perspective of Tribal Development," The Communication Barrier in Tribal Development (ed. Prabhakar Nanda, P.C. Mohapatro and J. Samal), Das Brothers 1991 pp. 2, 3 (Berhampur).
2. B.D. Sharma, D.O. Letter No, 1/Gen/90 -R U III. Dated. 28.5.90. Commissioner for Scheduled Castes and Scheduled Tribes, addressed to President of India is quoted by K.C. Panigrahy in 'Fundamentals of An Approach to the Tribes, October, Nov, December, 1997, Koraput p. 77.
3. Prof. Sanat T. Joshi, "Land Alienation and Accelerating Tribal Transformation", "Tribals in India The Changing Scenario", S.N. Tripathy (Ed.)Discovery Publishing House, 1998 (p. 11).
4. R.K. Paney "Institutional Finance for Agriculture in India" Ashish Publishing House, New Delhi (p. 19).
5. Eswar Rao Patnaik "Problems and Prospects of Agricultural Development in Koraput district unpublished Thesis p. 140.
6. P.C. Mohapatro, "Economic Development of Tribal India" Ashish Publishing House, New Delhi 1985.
7. Nanavati, B. Manilal and Anjaria, J : The Indian Rural Problem, Vora and Co Publishers Ltd. Bombay, 1947 p. 221.
8. District Statistical Hand Book, 1989-90, Koraput, p. 8.
9. Belshaw Horace : Agricultural Credit in Economically under-developed countries, F.J.A.O (U.N.), Rome, 1959 p. 229.

10. Kumar Sunil : Commercial Banks and Rural Development, Kurukshetra, March, 1987, p. 40.
11. S. Jagannathan, Governor, R.B.I., Functions and working, 1970, p. 10.
12. Jathar, G.B. and K.J. Jathar, Indian Economy, Oxford University Press, 1957, London, p. 128.
13. Patnaik, Sarish, Agricultural credit development, *Indian Express*, July, 1989, p. 1.
14. Rao, P.S, *The Hindu*, May, 28, 1988, p. 5.
15. Mukherjee, S., Mohapatro, P.C. and Patnaik Eswar Rao, Economic survey of selected villages of Koraput district, Vani Mudrani, 1988 Jeypore, p. 6.
16. R.C.S. Bell, Orissa District Gazetters, 1941, Government Press, Cuttack, p. 16.
17. World Development Report, Oxford University Press, London 1986, p. 98.

The author recounts his interview with the then Collector of Koraput district, Sri Rabi Narayana Senapati, who said the stagnation of tribals which persisted over centuries can not be overcome overnight.

The scholar is indebted to Dr. P.C. Mohapatro, Reader in Economics, D.A.V. College, Koraput for his effective supervision of this scholar in completion of the thesis.

7

Co-Operatives for Tribal Development in Orissa

Dr. S.N.Tripathy*

The tribals in India, as well as in Orissa, live in forests, hills and naturally isolated regions. Eighty per cent of the tribals in India are concentrated in the central belt which extends from Gujarat, Rajasthan to West Bengal encompassing the states of Maharashtra, Madhya Pradesh, Andhra Pradesh, Bihar and Orissa.

According to 1991 census, Orissa has more than 70.34 lakhs tribal population of which nearly 35.15 lakhs are males and 35.19 lakhs are females. The district Koraput, Mayurbhanj, Sundargarh, Kalahandi and Phulbani are mostly tribal dominated.[1]

The backwardness of tribal regions, widespread poverty of the tribals and problems of integrating them with the mainstream of civilisation, etc., are stumbling blocks in the path of tribal development.

To get into a micro-situation of tribal districts or Orissa, we find a wide disparity between the coastal districts and hilly tribal

* *Dr. Tripathy belongs to the department of Economics, Aska Science College, Aska (Orissa)*

regions. There are economic disparities, social variations, demographic differences, educational levels, migration patterns, consumption standards or technological gaps between the tribal regions and coastal regions.[2]

The tribals of Orissa, with slight variations have a highly egalitarian society, with high status for women, dignity of labour. They have maintained their values as manifested in their rites and rituals, traditional institutions, in spite of centuries of onslaughts of external forces.[3]

CONSTITUTIONAL AND LEGISLATIVE PROVISIONS

The constitution provides for a comprehensive frame work for the socio-economic development of tribals and for preventing their exploitation by other groups of society. Article 46 of the constitution requires the state (both central and state Governments) to promote with special care the educational and economic interests of the weaker sections and specially tribals and to protect them from social injustice and all forms of exploitation.

To curb exploitation of the tribals several protective regulations have been enacted from time to time and subsequently ammended to cope up with the changing situations. Accordingly, in addition to the general laws, specific regulations have been enacted to safeguard the interests of the tribals. Noteworthy among them are :

(i) The Orissa Scheduled areas transfer of immovable (by Scheduled Tribes) Regulation, 1956.

(ii) The Orissa Land Reforms Act, 1960.

(iii) The Orissa (Scheduled areas) Money-lenders, Regulation, 1967.

(iv) Orissa (Scheduled areas) Debt Relief Regulation 1967.

(v) The Bonded Labour System (Abolition) Act, 1976.

(vi) The Orissa Reservation of vacancies in posts and services (for Scheduled Castes and Scheduled Tribes).

However, despite these enactments, large numbers among tribals remained in the grip of widespread poverty and exploitation.

Inaccessibility of many tribal regions, inadequate facilities of assessing the impact of many development programmes on the tribal life and corruption at every stage of plan implementation has resulted in the backwardness and poverty of the tribals.

It has been aptly remarked, "one of the most striking experiences of planned development in India has been that economically backward areas have gained little from the planning."[4]

MARKETING OF TRIBAL PRODUCE

Mostly tribal marketing consists of supplying the minor products and some typical products collected from the forest. The tribal people like the Kutias of Belghar region of Phulbani district in Orissa mainly supply agricultural products like Jhudunga (cow peas), Kandulo (hill grams), mustard seeds. They also sell forest products like hill brooms, siali leaves, sal seeds and kusumo seeds.[5]

Co-operatives were introduced in the tribal areas to improve the socio-economic conditions of the tribals and to save them from the exploitation of money lenders and traders. Large-sized-multipurpose co-operative societies (LAMPS) and Regional Marketing Co-operative Societies (RMCS) are started in tribal areas in order to save the tribals from exploitation in marketing and credit front. The entry of co-operatives in the tribal market has enabled the tribal communities not only to improve their bargaining capacity, but also to secure a more lucrative price for their produce.[6]

In the light of aforesaid analysis, it is imperative to high-light the role of the Agency Marketing Co-operative Society (AMCS) for the development of Phulbani tribals (Orissa). The district Phulbani has a total population of 5,46,000 out of which SC and ST population constitute 18.3 per cent and 51.4 per cent respectively as per 1991 census. We can review the role of AMCS on the basis of the data collected from the Annual Administrative Reports of AMCS, Tikabali (Phulbani).

The Agency Marketing Co-operative Society Ltd., has started 75 collection centres at various places in Phulbani (undivided) in order to collect minor forest produce and agricultural products from the tribals. The purchase and sales of the AMCS during the period 1991-92 to 1994-95 has been analysed in Table 7.1 and Table 7.2.

TABLE 7.1

Sl. No.	*Commodities purchased*	*1991-92 Rs.*	*1992-93 Rs.*	*1993-94 Rs.*	*1994-95 Rs.*
1.	Minor forest products.	1,61,49,148	1,82,40,065	2,21,62,400	1,83,48,082
2.	Agricultural products.	5,33,561	3,29,941	3,07,869	2,57,363
3.	Consumer goods	5,19,613	5,25,738	4,26,830	2,20,031
Total		1,72,02,322	1,90,95,743	2,28,97,099	1,88,25,476

A close observation of Table 7.1 reveals that there has been an erratic trend of purchase of minor forest products and Agricultural products in Phulbani. However, the purchase of Consumer goods by AMCS exhibits an increasing trend during the period under review.

TABLE 7.2

Sl. No.	*Commodities*	*1991-92 Rs.*	*1992-93 Rs.*	*1993-94 Rs.*	*1994-95 Rs.*
1.	Minor forest products.	2,06,62,785	2,79,53,550	3,58,18,692	2,99,85,814
2.	Agricultural products.	1,12,722	5,43,692	19,228	7,82,610
3.	Consumer goods	7,20,346	6,24,964	3,90,015	2,66,542
Total		2,14,95,853	2,91,22,206	3,62,27,935	3,10,34,966

Source : Annual Administrative Reports of AMCS Ltd, Tikabali (Orissa).

Table 7.2 depicts that the sale of minor forest produce has shown an increased trend up to 1993-94 and it has declined in 1994-95. The sale of agricultural product as well as consumer goods has recorded a fluctuating trend during period under study.

It is heartening to note that the AMCS has made profits to the tune of Rs. 32,41,267 in the year 1994-95.

Notwithstanding the aforesaid facts, it has been observed that the Government institutions mostly consisting of the co-operatives have been able to procure only about 10 per cent of the total market arrivals of minor forest produce and surplus agricultural products. It is also found that there has been fluctuation in collection of tribal products by the Government agencies. Even the institutional agencies have not made payments to tribals in better terms than the private trader for collection of their minor forest produce and agricultural products.[7]

Therefore, it is imperative to bring the tribals under the co-operative fold not only to relieve them from the clutches of the private money lenders-cum-traders but also to ameliorate the living standards of the tribals by fair price payment through co-operatives.

Active participation of the tribal members in co-operatives is required for the successful procurement of tribal produce and marketable surplus. The procurement price should be remunerative to the tribal cultivators which would boost up production and alleviate poverty among the exploited tribals of Orissa.

There should be facilities of credit-cum-marketing to halt the process of tribal exploitation consequent upon distressed payment of tribal products by money lenders and middle-men.

REFERENCES

1. Tripathy, S.N., *Tribals in India: The Changing Scenario,* Discovery Publishing House, New Delhi, (1998) p. 403 (Edited)
2. Tripathy, S.N., *Impact of Road Transport in Tribal India,* Discovery Publishing House, New Delhi (1994) p.137.
3. *Ibid.*
4. National Council of Applied Economic Research. New Delhi 'Survey of Backward Districts of Orissa', p.1.
5. Tripathy, S.N., *Tribals in India. The Changing Scenario. Op. cit.* p. 342.
6. Mahalingam, S., *Role of Co-operative Organisations in Developing Tribal Economy,* Mittal Publications, New Delhi, 1990, p. 118.
7. Satapathy, T., Marketing Strategy in Tribal Developing Planning in Orissa—An Appraisal. *Orissa Economic Journal,* Vol.I, XVII. 1985, p. 71.

8

Role of Tribal Development Cooperative Corporation in Orissa

Dr. P.C. Samantarary*

INTRODUCTION

The tribal situation in India presents a varied and a complex picture and poses peculiar problems of economic development. India has got the largest concentration of tribal population in the world, next to Africa. According to 1991 census, the total population of the country stood at 843.93 million out of which Scheduled Tribe was found to be 67.76 million (excluding Jammu and Kashmir) which constitute roughly 8.08 per cent of the total population of the country, which means one tribesmen for every 13 Indians. Areas inhabited by tribals constitute a significant part of the backward areas of the country. On the whole it is estimated that the predominant tribal areas comprise of about 15 per cent of the total geographical area of the country. Their main concentrations are the central tribal belt in middle India and in the north-east. About 50 per cent of the tribal population of the country is concentrated in the state of Madhya Pradesh, Bihar and Orissa. Besides, there is a sizable tribal population in Maharashtra, Gujarat, Rajasthan and West Bengal.

* *Vice Principal, Regional Institute of Cooperative Management, Bangalore.*

In Orissa, the Scheduled Tribes with a population of 70,32,214 (1991 census) constitute 22.36 per cent of the total population of the state which occupies third place next to Maharashtra and Madhya Pradesh. The state contains 62 varieties of either groups out of 283 numbers of Scheduled Tribes in the country. The Scheduled Tribes are distributed in almost all the districts of the state in varying proportions. In certain districts, like undivided Koraput, Sundargarh and Mayurbhanja their concentration is very high exceeding in each case more than half of the total population of the district. Among the tribal groups some communities, like the Kandha, the Gond and the Santal are very large and widely distributed, while others like the Chenchu, the Bondo are very small in number and found concentrated in certain pockets only. They are living mostly in the thick forests, on hillslopes and plateau with poor natural resources.

Among the tribal groups the rural dwellers and urban dwellers constitute 94.8 per cent and 5.2 per cent, respectively. The sex ratio among them is 1002 females per 1000 males as against the state figure of 992. The growth rate among them during the period (1981-91) is 18.89 per cent in comparison with 20.15 per cent of the whole state. The percentage of literacy among them is 18.10 which is far below the state figure of 44.08. The district-wise distribution of tribal population shows that in terms of proportion of Scheduled Tribe population to total population the district Mayurbhanja with 57.87 per cent occupies the first position and Cuttack with 3.30 per cent lies at the bottom. Similarly, on the basis of percentage of tribal population of the district to total population of the state, Koraput (Undivided) comes first with 23.27 per cent and Puri with 1.8 per cent occupies the lowest position. On the basis of the numerical strength there are 15 major tribal groups each having more than one lakh population. Among the tribal groups 13 ethnic groups have been identified as Primitive Tribal Groups (PTGs).

ORIGIN

Etymologically, the term tribe, derives its origin from the word "tribuz" meaning three divisions. For Romans the tribe was a political division. A tribe occupies definite geographical area and exercise effective control over its people. Permanent settlement in a particular area gives geographical identity to the tribe. The territory under the domain of a particular tribe was generally named after it. It is believed that India derives its name Bharat from the mighty BHARATA tribe. Similarly, the vast Matsya kingdom which flourished in the sixth century B.C. was identified with the MATSYA tribe. The Mina tribe from Rajasthan and Madhya Pradesh is believed to be the descendant of the Matsya tribe.

The Mina's believe that Matsya or Meena, i.e., the Fish is the origin of this universe.

Even today there are a number of regions which owe their names to the tribes inhabiting them. The states of Mizoram, Nagaland and Tripura are named after the Mizo, Naga and Tripura tribes respectively.

SOCIO-ECONOMIC PROFILE

The tribals in Orissa have continued to remain socially, economically and educationally backward and are languishing at the bottom of socio-economic ladder. For generations together they are residing in inaccessible forest and hilly areas. They prefer to live in total isolation of the public and are fully secluded from the main stream of the population. Their geographical isolation and impoverished economy have made them object of exploitive economic and trade practices of non-tribals living or entering the tribal areas. Considering certain broad features, like ecological-geographical set up of the tribal areas traditional economy and level of skill, socio-cultural traditions, current process of modernization and enculturization the tribes of Orissa can be classified as (1) Hunters, and food gatherers, (2) Cattle-herders and gatherers, (3) Simple artisans and gatherers, (4) Shifting cultivators, herders and gatherers, (5) Settled agriculturists, herders and gatherers (6) Industrial and urban workers. Except the people belonging to the last category who have left their traditional set up and migrated to a new kind of sophisticated setting in search of employment, all others of the rest five categories though differ from one another in terms of their primary occupation, held one thing in common, i.e., the collection of minor forest produce. However, the degree of dependence on forest varies from group to group based on its availability near by.

TRIBAL DEVELOPMENT STRATEGY

Tribal population and development are inter-dependent. In fact we cannot conceive of development in a vacuum. Development is a very broad term which encompasses various changes that are taking place due to human intervention. During the British period the tribals were completely neglected due to the policy of "leave them alone". This isolation has deprived them of the fruits of scientific and technological advances leading to their distinctive life-styles, cultures and languages. To eliminate the age old exploitation and repression of tribals in different economic activities, sincere efforts have been made by the Government in building up co-operative structure in the tribal economy during the plan period in India. Many commissions, committees, study teams and working groups have repeatedly been emphasised the significance of co-operativization of tribal economy in the country. In its report, the social welfare team of the committee on plan projects(1959) recommended that, "Commercial exploitation of forests be entrusted to co-operatives rather than to contractors. The Dhebar Commission (1961) recommended that "the sale and marketing of the produce and supply of tribal peoples' requirements at reasonable price should receive special attention through cooperatives. A Special Working Group on Cooperation (1961) attributed the slow development of cooperative movement in tribal areas to structural weakness, operational defects, management problems, faculty procedures and business methods which are not possible to the tribals. The group suggested a separate organisational set up for promotion of cooperative ideas among the tribal communities, so as to provide such services as were being rendered by private traders and further recommended the formation of an "Integrated Service Cooperative Society" at haat level. As a result of the recommendations of the Working Group, State Governments set up Forest Labour Cooperative societies and multi-purpose co-operative societies and State level Tribal Development Corporations. Further, to improve the operational efficiency of co-operatives in Tribal Areas, a Committee on co-operative structure in Tribal Areas under the Chairmanship of K.S. Bawa (1971) has recommended for the organisation of the Large Scale Adivasi Multi-purpose Societies (LAMPS) by amalgamating service cooperative. societies (SCS) in tribal areas which include package of services for tribal people. The main components of this package are credit (both production and consumption), supply of seeds and other agricultural inputs, marketing of agricultural and minor forest produce and supply of consumer goods. The committee recommended that a tribesman should not be required to approach too many institutions for assistance and the co-operative structure should essentially provide integrated credit and other services at one point. They suggested for creation of LAMPS at block level with branches at G.P. Headquarters or at important weekly market/Haat centres. For credit purposes the LAMPS have to be serviced by the Central Cooperative Banks (CCB), for supply of inputs and marketing and agricultural produce to the Regional Co-operative Marketing Society (RCMS) and for marketing of minor forest produce (MFP) to the Tribal Development Co-operative Society.

ROLE OF TRIBAL DEVELOPMENT COOPERATIVE CORPORATION

With this back drop the Tribal Development Cooperative Corporation of Orissa Ltd., as an apex organisation was registered in the year 1973 having extended its area of operation throughout the state. The corporation stands for protecting the interest of tribal people in the field of procuring and marketing their agricultural produce including Minor Forest Produce (MFP).

OBJECTIVES

The Tribal Development Co-operative Corporation Ltd. (TDCC) aims at development of the tribal communities of the state through elimination of their economic exploitation by the unscrupulous middlemen and private traders. The main objectives of the study is as follows:

1. To examine the activities of TDCC and to know how it procures Surplus Agricultural Produce (SAP) and Minor Forest Produce (MFP)

2. To study its marketing activities and how it arranges for marketing

3. To assess its consumer activities through fair price shops

4. To find out its problems and suggest remedial measures.

MEMBERSHIP

The membership composition of the corporation at present, includes 203 LAMPS, 35 other primary cooperative societies, 47 Panchayat Samities, State Government and 3 individuals. Out of the total 30 districts of Orissa, it has already covered 2/3 of the districts. The registered office is located at Bhubaneswar with a wide net-work comprising 3 Divisional offices functioning at Berhampur, Sunabeda and Keonjhar, 15 branch offices 150 permanent procurement centres and 79 Fair price shops covering entire tribal region of the state. It has also 66 godowns located at different places with a storage capacity of 35998 M.T.

FINANCIAL POSITION

The authorised share capital of the corporation is Rs. 20.00 crores against which the paid up share capital as on 31.8.97 is Rs. 1626.19 lakhs which is detailed as under.

	(Rs. in lakhs)
1. State Government in H and T.W. Department	1305.17
2. Government of India in the Ministry of Welfare	200.00
3. State Government in A and C Department	19.25
4. Co-operative Societies	1.46
5. Panchayat Samities	30.12
6. State Government in H and T.W Department participation in PSFS scheme	39.89
Total	1626.19

The financial assistance in the shape of share capital investment, grants-in-aid, subsidies and managerial assistance from State Government are in the tune of 1350.72, 335.90, 64.758 and 208.95 (Rupees in lakhs) respectively. The borrowings of the corporation from different sources as on 1996-97 stands to be Rs. 1758.18 lakhs.

FUNCTIONING

The corporation through its branches has taken up collection of SAP and MFP directly from the tribals. Among the SAP the items of collection include niger, mustard, gingerly, ragi, jawar, maize, paddy, pulses and turmeric. Among the MFP the procured items include tamarind, sal seed, myrobalam, sal and siali leaves, mahua flowers, hill brooms, arrowroot marketing cleaning nuts, honey, sabaigrass, etc. The marketing activities mainly constitutes the said items. To add to this the corporation has been granted lease of minor forest produces in 19 forests divisions from the year 1991 out of 27 territorial divisions in the state. In respect of certain items of MFP, the TDCC has been granted exclusive right of collection.

In addition to its own staff in the "Haats" and villages, TDCC also opens temporary procurement centre at different remote tribal areas to purchase SAP and MFP from the tribals. Besides, Fair price (FP) shops also function as procurement centres in busy seasons. Every year nearly 800 temporary centres are opened in tribal areas for taking business. In addition to the above arrangements, the LAMPS and other co-operatives also function as agents of TDCC for procurement of MFP and SAP. Taking into account the SAP and MFP procurement the business turnover of the TDCC for the last 5 years is described as under.

TABLE 8.1
PROCUREMENT OF SAP AND MFP BY TDCC (RS. IN LAKHS)

Year	*Procurement*		*Consumer business*	*Total*
	SAP	*MFP*		
1992-93	429.63	221.00	141.13	791.86
1993-94	90.69	321.83	187.51	599.26
1994-95	250.45	330.00	300.47	880.92
1995-96	318.52	338.24	367.95	1024.71
1996-97	278.44	255.43	380.08	917.95

(*Source*: Annual Report of TDCC 1996-97).

Table 8.1 reveals that procurement of SAP and MFP items during 1992-93 was quite encouraging and the total business including consumer activities stood at Rs. 791.86 lakhs. in the year 1993-94 the business declined to Rs. 599.26 lakhs. Further, in the year 1994-95 and 1995-96 its business has gone up to the tune of Rs. 880.42 and Rs.1024.71 lakhs respectively unfortunately, again the business declined due to heavy losses during the year 1996-97.

Owing to the continuous losses sustained by this corporation its share capital has been completely eroded and the business activities at present are carried on by borrowings and forward sale arrangements. The borrowings from different sources during the year 1996-97 stands at Rs. 1758.18 lakhs.

PROFIT AND LOSS POSITION

The year wise profit and loss position of the corporation from 1991-92 to 1995-96 is given below:

TABLE 8.2
PROFIT AND LOSS POSITION AT THE TDCC

Year	Gross Profit (+) Loss (-)	NetProfit/Loss
1991-92	(-) 645.92	(-) 984.81
1992-93	(-) 39.15	(-) 506.81
1993-94	(+) 81.82	(-) 340.25
1994-95	(+) 100.52	(-) 285.94
1995-96	(-) 40.75	(-) 324.86

From Table 8.2 it is evident that in spite of earning profit on trading account the corporation is sustaining net loss due to various fall ons beyond the control of the management. The major losses may be due to (a) heavy interest burden on borrowing (b) high over head expenditure (c) market fluctuation/constraints and (d) high cost of management.

PROBLEMS

The major problems faced by TDCC over the years are as follows:

1. Quantity of procurement of produce is very inadequate, and whatever the items procured by the tribals, owing to transport problems unable to supply it to TDCC in time and as such the middlemen enjoy the benefit at less price.

2. Local traders purchase from tribals on outright basis during the harvest season and TDCC being an apex organisation its lengthy official procedure jeopardises its business.

3. Too much Government interference in case of fixing the procurement price of SAPs and MFPs adds to the problem.

4. TDCC does not have its storage facilities as a result of which it would not procure even when things are available at low price.

5. TDCC to procure the forest produces is not free from paying loyalty to the state government like other TDCCs functioning in the country.

6. TDCC has not been able to get an absolute lease for procuring the minor forest produces and

7. The establishment cost of TDCC is much higher than the managerial subsidies received from the government.

SUGGESTIONS

As a remedial measure the following points are to be taken care so as to enable TDCC to overcome the above problems.

1. The TDCC has to fix up the procurement price of the SAPs and MFPs without government interference.

2. The TDCC must be given adequate funds for the construction of its godowns and cold storage.

3. Absolute lease may be given to the TDCC only , which being an apex body will act as catalyst to procure minor forest produces and expand its marketing activities in a diversified manner.

4. The state government may either exempt the royalty to the TDCC or shoulder its entire establishment cost and

5. The state government should make a detailed study of the functioning of TDCC in procurement and marketing of tribal produce and initiate suitable measures to re-establish their effectiveness.

CONCLUSION

The economic activities of the tribals have to be linked to the restructuring of the TDCC is a first step towards the tribal peoples' participation in their own empowerment. An integrated approach is needed if the tribal people are to claim their rightful place in the state economy. The main problems of the tribals is their ignorance, illiteracy, rigid adherence to traditional faiths, poverty, etc., encourage others to exploit them. Dispassionately we have to conceptualise that cooperation, which is very much a part and parcel of the tribal ethos, is to be sensitised through vital tribal social institutions which are not extant overtime. These social institutions as self-help groups/ units and good quality NGOs to be encouraged to come forward to take up the work in these areas so as to enable the tribals to overcome their bottlenecks for the cause of their socio economic development.

REFERENCES

1. Das, Banabehari, "Economic upliftment of Tribals; Role of Cooperatives", *The Co-operator*, Vol. xvii, No. 23 June, 1980.
2. Dr. Mahalingam, S., "Marketing of Agricultural produces through Tribal Cooperatives—Replica of Tawang Model in North-East India". *Journal of Rural Development*, Hyderabad, volume. iv March 1991.
3. Pattanaik, B.K., "Review of Impact of Cooperatives on Tribals' life in Orissa", *Indian Co-operative Review*, New Delhi, vol. xii, No. 2, Jan. 1975.
4. Robert Goodland *et al.*, Tribal peoples and Economic Development, The International Bank for Reconstruction and Development, New York, May, 1982.
5. Census of India, 1991
6. Government of India, Report of the study team on credit, marketing and cooperation in Tribal Areas during medium term plan 1978-83, Ministry of Home Affairs, New Delhi, May 1978.
7. Government of India, Report of the Commissioner for Scheduled Castes and Scheduled Tribes, Part-I, 1979-80 and 1980-81.
8. Government of India, Report of the working group on Tribal Development, (1985-90) Planning Commission, New Delhi.
9. Annual/Audit Report of TDCC 1995-96 and 1996-97.
10. Annual statistical report of RCS, Orissa, 1995-96 and 1996-97.

9

Human Resource Development in Tribal Areas of Gujarat

Dr. M.I. Masavi*

INTRODUCTION

Education enriches life and helps an individual to develop his personality. It sharpens intellectual faculties, builds character and creates proper social and intellectual climate by arousal of curiosity, adventure and social aspirations in a progressive community. It is concerned with both the common welfare and the development and personal satisfaction of individuals.[1] The latest researches have shown that the large part of the national income growth in the industrialised nations is not possible without education.[2]

The education programmes help to train the people to place responsibilities before rights. The educational system should also satisfy the cultural heads, which is essential for the healthy growth of the nation. The system of education has also a determining influence on the rate at which economic progress is achieved and the benefits which can be derived from it. Economic development naturally makes growing demands on human resources and in a

* *Deputy Director, Tribal Research and Training Institute, Gujarat Vidyapith Ahmedabad - 380 014*

democratic set-up it calls for values and attitudes in the building of which the quality of education is an important element.[3] During the planned period education was regarded as the most important single factor in achieving rapid economic development and technological progress and in creating a social order founded on the values of freedom, social justice and equal opportunity. Fourth Five Year Plan underlined the relation between education can facilitate and promote social change and contribute to economic growth, not only by training skilled manpower for specific tasks of development, but what is perhaps even more important, by creating the requisite attitudes and climate.[4] Economic development of an area and social welfare of its people depend largely on the optimum utilisation of human resources and in building up of this resource, education plays a vital role as it brings return in the form of skilled manpower geared to the needs of development.

The importance of education as an agency of modernisation as well as source of employment has long been realised in India's national plans for tribal welfare. A great portion of the grants both from the State and Central sectors have been invested for improving education in primary, secondary and higher education levels. However, the wastage and drop-outs in tribal areas have been stupendous. Owing to this, the desired benefits have been drawn only by such sections of the tribes which were prepared to take advantage from this programme. A perusal of the reports by different committees on tribal welfare highlights varying degree of emphasis on the two important sectors, viz., economic development and education. While the former argues that the tribal world is ridden with poverty and needs means of surviving, in the case of the later, the argument is that the tribal people are mostly backward because they are least educated and education should get first priority.[5]

The constitution of India provides as Directive Principle of State Policy that the state should promote with special care the educational and economic interests of the weaker sections of the people and in particular, of the tribes and should protect them from social injustice and all forms of exploitation.[6]

It is of late that the role of education as an investment in human resources has been increasingly recognised all over the developing countries. Although the spread of education in India as a whole has been quite fast in the last four decades, the spread of education amongst the Scheduled Tribes has been quite uneven. It is in this context that a national policy was adopted which aimed at 100 per cent enrolment in the age-group of 6-11 by the year 1978-79, and 50 per cent enrolment in the age-group of 11-14 by that date. In 1973, the Standing Committee of the Central Advisory Board of Education agreed that 'Every effort should be made at the elementary level, to enrol all children of Scheduled Castes and Scheduled Tribes'. Every State Government should propose specific targets for the purpose of this. All necessary steps for the purpose should be taken. These would include the tribal languages, orientation of teachers in tribal language, provision of special allowances and other facilities to teachers working in tribal areas, free supply of educational materials, clothing or mid-day meals, provision of scholarships and hostel where necessary, increasing number of Ashram Schools, etc. The funds required for these programmes should be provided in the general sector on a priority basis.[8]

THE TRIBAL SCENARIO

The tribal population in the State accounts for about 15% of the Gujarat population as per 1991 Census. In absolute terms, it is 6.2 millions. Gujarat State occupies 5th position (8%) in the country in matter of tribal population followed by Madhya Pradesh, Orissa. Bihar and Maharashtra. The entire Eastern belt of the State comprises of the tribal population. Out of 19 districts in the State, 8 districts have sizeable tribal population. Besides 8 districts usually referred as tribal districts, there are some tribal pocket in Junagadh, Kutch, Jamnagar and Ahmedabad districts. However, only 8 districts have been included area under tribal sub-plan for the purpose of planning and development programmes for the tribal population. The post Fifth Plan categorised the tribal population into three groups. First group consists of tribals in ITDP areas while the second group consists of dispersed tribals living predominantly in non-tribal areas or urban areas. The primitive tribal group comprising of very backward tribals make the third group. There are five tribes identified as primitive tribal group, viz., Kotdalia, Kolgha/Kathodi, Padhar and Siddis. There are 28 tribal communities covered in the scheduled lists of tribes in the State. There is a great disparity among the tribal groups in the level of socio-economic development. Among some of the tribes, such as, Dhodia, Chaudhry, Patelias and Dangri Garasias the process of socio-economic chause appear too rapid leading to the extent of decentralisation and detribalisation. By and large there is no significant chause in economic conditions of most of the tribal communities. A vast majority of them have still remain under developed with high incidence of poverty.

The economic backwardness as also the educational backwardness, the two major ills are primarily responsible for the overall backwardness of tribal communities. To bring speedy improvement in both these spheres the Government of India and the State Government are making large scale concerned efforts. It is generally accepted that spread of education among the tribal communities is an essential pre-requisite to their economic development and therefore, all possible efforts are being spent by government. In view of various educational facilities and concessions available at present a tribal boy or girl can aspire to reach the highest ladder of education for which he or she need not face any kind of financial difficulties. On account of these facilities, there have been a rapid expansion in the number of tribal students at all stages of education in the Gujarat State. The Government of Gujarat has made a great stride in the development of education in the State.

Table 9.1 gives a comparative statistical picture of literacy rate by sex and area in Gujarat and India. It can be seen that Gujarat in 1981 and 1991 had a higher literacy rate.

TABLE 9.1
LITERACY RATE BY SEX AND AREA

	Gujarat		*India*	
	Census 1981	*1991*	*Census 1981*	*1991*
Male	65%	73%	56.4%	64%
Female	38.5	48.6	29.8	39.3
Total	52.2	61.3	45.7	52.1
Rural	43.6	53.1	36.1	44.5
Urban	71.0	76.5	67.3	73.0

Source : Census of India, 1981, 1991.

Table 9.1 shows that the literacy rate in Gujarat for males was 73% in 1991 and females was 48.6% against respective All India figures 64.1 and 39.3 per cent.

TRIBAL LITERACY

The general literacy rate amongst the S.T. in Gujarat according to Census was 11.69 in 1961, 14.12 in 1971, and 21.14 in 1981 which is raised to 29.67 in 1991 against the general literacy rate of 51.15 in the State and 50.49 per cent in SC population. As there is wide gap in the literacy rate as various schemes are in operation. Besides various incentives for education, such as opportunity cost to most backward tribes, etc., have been provided, so that tribal students may be included to have better education.

Table 9.2 shows the Literacy Rates of Gujarat for SC and ST for 1961,1971,1981 and 1991.

TABLE 9.2: LITERACY RATE OF GUJARAT, SC, ST FOR 1961, 1971, 1981 AND 1991

Category	*Census Year*			
	1961	1971	1981	1991
Male	41.13	46.11	54.44	60.99
Female	19.10	24.75	32.33	40.62
Total :	30.45	35.79	43.70	51.15
SC Male	34.83	30.89	53.14	62.32
SC Female	10.73	14.95	25.61	37.71
SC Total :	22.46	27.74	39.79	50.49
ST Male	19.06	21.83	30.41	39.37
ST Female	4.03	6.15	11.64	19.65
ST Total :	11.69	14.12	21.14	29.67

Table 9.2 indicates the statistics pertaining to literacy rate for tribals for 1961-71-81 and 91. The noteworthy feature is that over the whole period difference between male and females is gradually diminishing. But compared to general and SC population the tribals are far behind in education. There is a wide inequality in ST female literacy with SC general female literacy. Only one-fifth of the tribal women population are literate.

Looking to the level of literacy in different tribal groups there is wide inequality among them. The statistical data pertaining to literacy in different tribal groups is in Appendix-I. There are considerable differences in the literacy rates among tribals as per 1981 Census. Besides, Gonds, Raj, Patelias, Dhodias, Bavchas and Chaudhries are more literate while Charans, Koli, Padhar, Pardhi, Rabari, Vaghri, Warli, Kathodi, Kolgha, and Bhil may be considered quite illiterate which has deep implications for the social context in terms of creating social hierarchy among tribal groups.

WASTAGE AND STAGNATION

As wastage and stagnation has been the most significant features, several scholars and researchers have attempted to analyse these two issues in the context of tribal communities. It should be mentioned that most of the studies related with tribal education in Gujarat pertain to tribal education in general studies related specifically with primary education of girls and tribal children are very few. As a matter of fact most of the studies are undertaken by Tribal Research Institute of Gujarat Vidyapith, Ahmedabad alone in the State. Lal, R.B., studied wastage and stagnation in primary education in tribal areas in 1967-68. This was followed by the studies conducted by Masavi for the year 1967-68 and 1969-70 pertaining to both Panchayat Schools and Ashram Schools. A similar study was done by Bharti Desai and Anil Patel in 1981 for Ashram Schools. Masavi and Arun Patel examined the wastage in low literacy areas in Gujarat in 1990. This was coupled with a study by Arun Patel of wastage in primary education in the tribal areas of almost Zero level literacy. The aforesaid studies were case studies and based on authors own surveys and methodology.

Various factors emerged as responsible for high incidence of wastage and stagnation from those studies. The foremost being the lack of adequate consciousness among the older generation for the need of formal education. Next important factor was found to be poor economic conditions of the large majority of tribals to the effect that every member of the family, young or old had to contribute towards sustaining the family. Children of school going age had either to look after younger babies in the family or to go to tend cattle and thus had economic value which did not permit them to go to school. Another significant cause for high incidence of wastage and stagnation was the inadequate, inefficient and insincere role played by teachers. Masavi in his study pointed out that the drop-out rate among the day scholars is much higher as compared to that among the inmates of Ashram Schools. There are many personal and family reasons for more number of girls discontinuing their education midway. Attainment of poverty and getting ready for marriage, meagre employment opportunities for women are a few other reasons indicated.

CONCLUSIONS

The very low level of technological developments existing in the tribal areas when compared and contrasted with the educational advancement and confidence gained by the City lads through the educational process need to be assessed in the proper perspectives and contexts through the time scale. It is thus necessary to chalk out a working system of need-based education which would help the tribal children acquire more confidence in dealing with their own environment first and then it would be easier to lead them to the path of formal education. This would also reduce the present migration to cities of maze ways in search of non-existing employment opportunities.

APPENDIX
LEVEL OF LITERACY AMONG DIFFERENT TRIBAL GROUPS.

	Male		Female		Total		%Increase
	1971	1981	1971	1981	1971	1981	
Gujarat	21.83	30.41	6.15	11.64	14.12	21.14	7.02
Barda	40.00	48.59	5.56	29.91	28.30	40.42	12.12
Bhvcha	38.26	45.44	21.27	26.73	30.49	36.51	6.02
Bharvad	3.09	14.81	0.45	4.82	2.45	10.02	7.59
Bhil	19.43	27.85	3.90	8.24	11.73	18.18	6.45
Charan	1.79	9.03	0.25	1.75	1.06	5.54	4.48
Chaudhary	31.77	41.89	12.10	22.49	22.04	32.23	10.19
Dhanka	27.38	38.80	6.24	12.85	17.05	26.20	9.15
Dhodia	43.45	56.38	18.90	33.67	31.19	44.96	13.77
Dubala	20.96	25.87	6.32	9.73	13.74	17.92	4/18
Gamit	22.00	32.94	6.75	15.73	14.86	24.39	9.53
Gondas Raj	30.39	59.49	12.63	36.78	14.05	48.67	34.62
Kathodi	4.33	14.89	2.42	7.36	3.36	11.12	7.76
Konkana	19.27	29.05	5.30	10.62	12.56	19.94	7.38
Koli	5.26	9.89	0.32	1.11	2.87	5.71	2.84
Kolidhor	12.29	27.64	2.37	7.03	7.47	17.41	9.94
Kunbi	20.28	41.55	5.52	21.35	13.31	31.47	18.16
Naika	15.07	20.66	3.85	6.82	9.55	13.85	4.30
Padhar	3.99	11.38	0.09	1.51	2.08	6.57	4.49
Pardhi Kutch	7.88	12.40	1.45	2.43	4.88	7.47	2.59
Pardhi	23.17	32.47	15.68	9.28	21.88	21.40	-0.48
Patelia	32.74	42.47	4.23	9.51	18.94	36.36	17.42
Pomla	18.29	23.66	6.29	9.11	14.00	16.62	2.62
Rabari	4.42	9.29	0.27	2.64	2.43	6.04	3.61
Rathva	10.01	20.77	0.91	3.36	5.65	12.19	6.54
Siddi	23.28	35.06	6.02	1.81	14.82	23.04	8.22
Vaghri	5.38	6.33	0.17	0.73	2.92	3.57	0.65
Varli	8.85	15.42	1.13	4.30	5.03	9.87	4.84
Kotvalia	7.42	21.27	2.51	12.94	5.00	17.18	12.18

Source : Social Assessment Study—DPEP Gujarat
Sardar Patel Institute of Economic and Social Research, Ahmedabad, 1996.

REFERENCES

1. Roy J. Honewell, The educational work of Thomas Jefferson (Cambridge, 1931), p. 146.

2. Theodre W. Schultz, 'The Economic Value of Education (New York) 1963, p. 164.

3. Second Five Year Plan (New Delhi, 1956), p. 525.

4. Fourth Five Year Plan (New Delhi, 1969), p. 352.

5 Abdul A. Thahag: Planning for educational facilities in Tribal Areas—A case

study of Bastar District in M.P. Perspective on Tribal Development and Administration (Hyderabad 1975), p. 217.

6. Indian Constitution Article 46.
7. Om Mehta: Education for Scheduled Castes and Scheduled Tribes in India (New Delhi) 1974, p. 2.
8. *Ibid,* p.11.
9. Mustali Masavi, Gujarat Na Adivasio- (Statistical Analysis) Tribal Research and Training Inst. Guj. Vidyapith 1988, Pub. No. 157.
10. Mukund Trivedi, Niresshah, Mustali Masavi and Kanubhai Shah 'Social Assessment Study: DPEP of Gujarat' Sardar Patel Institute of Economic and Social Research, Ahmedabad, 1996.

10

Tribal Health and Development in Rajasthan

Dr. B.L. Nagda *

The tribal situation in India presents a varied and complex picture and poses peculiar problems of economic development. Demographically speaking, there are some 250 Scheduled Tribes with several sub-groups speaking some 100 languages/dialects. Most of these tribes constitute separate socio-cultural groups having distinct customs, traditions, marriage, kinship and property inheritance systems living largely in agricultural and pre-agricultural level of technology. There are food-gatherers, hunters, forest-land cultivators, shifting cultivators and minor forest produce collectors among these tribes. Their geographical isolation and impoverished economy have made them object of exploitative economic and trade practices of the non-tribals living in or entering the tribal areas.

Rajasthan, one of the most picturesque states of India is widely known for its lakes, places, deserts and the princely heritage and valour of the men. Its wide range of climate and topography makes it a challenging area to live in. Within the layout of the tourist fascination for the culture and beauty of Rajasthan lies the vulnerable

* *Assistant Director, Population Research Centre, Sukhadia University, Udaipur, 313 001.*

tribal group whose joys and hopes add brighter shades in places to otherwise gloomy but revealing portrait of tears and toil, suffering and sorrow of the quiet people who stand the shock of life's struggle in their voiceless way. The tribes of Rajasthan as elsewhere in the country are passing through a process of socio-cultural and demographic transformation. Demographic study of the tribal is a more recent development when some academic as well as administrative interest was generated owing to the phenomenon of the decline in the population of some tribes and subsequently increase in the others. Government from time to time chalk out effective welfare programme to give thrust and dynamism to the changing lifestyle of the tribes. But yet today the required level of development has not been achieved. According to 1991 Census, 8.08 per cent of the tribal population of India lives in Rajasthan forming 12.44 per cent of the total population of the State. Numerically, the Scheduled Tribe population is 5474881 (1991 Census) of which majority reside in rural areas—95.35 per cent.

The latest Census of India has revealed that there was 6.8 crore Scheduled Tribe population in the country which comprises nearly 8 per cent to the total population of the country. Whereas in the State of Rajasthan the 1991 census has enumerated nearly 55 lakhs persons as Scheduled Tribe. The proportion of the Scheduled Tribe population in the State of Rajasthan comprises 12 different groups, namely: Bhils, Bhil Meena, Damor, Dhanka, Garasia, Kathodi, Kokna, Koli, Dhor, Nayakda, Patelia Meena and Saharia. However, in terms of number, the major tribal communities in the State are Meena (49.88 per cent) Bhil (44.01 per cent) and Garasia (2.48 per cent).

Both Meena and Bheel together comprises nearly 94 per cent of the total Scheduled Tribe population of the State. Though the Scheduled Tribe population is found in all the 27 districts of the State but their major concentration as per the 1991 census has been found in the districts of Banswara (73.47 per cent), Dungarpur (65.84 per cent), Udaipur (31.79 per cent), Sirohi (23.39 per cent), Swaimadhopur (22.59 per cent), Bundi (20.25 per cent), Kota (14.20 per cent), Jhalawar (11.90 per cent), Tonk (11.89 per cent). For the remaining districts, the proportion was found less than 10 per cent to the total population of the district population. Significantly large proportion of the Scheduled population (nearly 95 per cent) reside in rural areas and around amongst them were found illiterate for the entire state of Rajasthan.

TRIBAL DEVELOPMENT STRATEGY

A total and comprehensive view of the tribal problem was first taken on the eve of the Fifth Plan (1974-79) when the latest strategy known as Tribal Sub-Plan strategy was evolved. The emphasis was not merely developmental but protective, not merely area-based, but with focus on the Scheduled Tribe population.

The broad approach of Tribal sub-Plan strategy was continued during the Sixth Plan period with greater emphasis on specific objectives, namely: (a) raising of productivity levels in production fields of tribals activities with a view of enabling a targeted number of families to go above the poverty line; (b) development of the human resources and upgradation of education; (c) elimination of exploitation of tribals in the field of alienation of land, money-lending, debt-bondage, trade, excise, forest; and (d) development of adequate infrastructure. By the end of this Plan period rich dividends of the new Tribal Sub-Plan strategy were reaped in the shape of a more integrated approach to planning and implementation, larger financial allocation both by the Centre and the States and considerably larger physical achievement in ammelioration of poverty of the targeted groups as also in the general and social service sectors.

Among the important contributions of the Tribal sub-Plan strategy over a period of years has been the gradual evolution of the concept of family-oriented programmes for eradication of poverty. The emphasis on family-oriented and beneficiary-oriented schemes during the Sixth Plan has had perceptible impact in substantially boosting up the number of tribal families economically assisted.

The long term objective of the Tribal Sub-Plan approach was to narrow the gap between the levels of development of tribal and other areas while improving the quality of life of the tribal communities. In brief, the approach envisaged in tackling the tribal problems has been by categorising them under three identifiable areas and groups :

(a) In regions of substantial tribal concentration, an area development approach is to be combined with a focus on the tribal population and their problems;

(b) In smaller areas of dispersed tribal population where the Scheduled Tribes live merged with the general population, a modified area approach on account of the truncated nature of the habitat, but with similar focus on the tribes, would be called for; and

(c) Certain extremely backward and smaller tribal groups living generally in pre-agricultural level of technology in inaccessible areas facing the problem of their very survival would be treated as a special category both within the areas of tribal concentration and outside and special group-oriented programmes would be formulated for them.

These three categories were brought respectively under Integrated Tribal Development Project (ITDP), Modified Area Development Approach (MADA) and Pockets and Primitive Tribe Projects.

LEVEL OF MORTALITY

Table 10.1 shows the mortality indicators of the respondents. The percentage of deaths was slightly higher in Minas (15.14%) in comparison to those of Bhils (14.55%). It is generally hypothesised that higher the fertility, higher would be the mortality. In Minas level of both fertility and mortality was higher than that of Bhils. The sex wise mortality did not reveal any uniform trend. In Bhils, female death was higher in comparison to male deaths, but reverse was the case in Minas.

The difference in mortality by sex was higher among Bhils than that of Minas. Jain (1996) has also pointed out that sex differentials in mortality is weak in India.

MORTALITY BY AGE

Age is an important aspect of analysis of mortality. Table

10.2 reveals the incidence of mortality by age and sex. It shows that a higher percentage of deaths was found in infants below the age of one year followed by children in age group 1-4 years in both, Bhils and Minas and the lowest percentage of deaths was in the ages of 15 years and above. This comparison reveals that infant morality was slightly higher in Minas than that of Bhils.

TABLE 10.1
MORTALITY INDICATORS

Indicator	*Bhil*			*Mina*		
	Male	Female	Total	Male	Female	Total
Total live births	389	381	770	445	427	872
Total deaths	53	59	112	68	64	132
Percentage of death by sex	47.32	52.68	100.00	51.52	48.48	100.00
Percentage of total death	13.62	15.49	14.55	15.28	14.99	15.14

TABLE 10.2
INCIDENCE OF MORTALITY BY AGE AND SEX

Age at death	Bhil			Mina		
	Male	Female	Total	Male	Female	Total
Less than one year	30 (56.61)	34 (57.63)	64 (57.14)	37 (54.41)	35 (54.69)	72 (54.54)
1-4	16 (30.19)	14 (23.73)	30 (26.78)	18 (26.47)	17 (26.56)	35 (26.52)
4-14	5 (9.43)	8 (13.56)	13 (11.61)	7 (10.30)	8 (12.50)	15 (11.36)
15 and above	2 (3.77)	3 (5.08)	5 (4.47)	6 (8.82)	4 (6.25)	10 (7.58)
Total	53 (100)	59 (100)	112 (100)	68 (100)	64 (100)	132 (100)

In case of child death and childhood death, variation between Bhils and Minas were very narrow. The percentage of deaths, in age above 15 years were higher in Minas than those in Bhils.

INFANT AND CHILD MORTALITY

The level of child mortality is always of interest both as an index of living conditions in the community and household and as a direct measure of family health. However, reliability of mortality estimates depends upon full recall of children who have died and accurate reporting of ages at death.

The sex differential of infant and child death is presented in Table 10.3. On the basis of death period of infants morality was divided into neo-natal and post-natal deaths of the children. The neo-natal death up to age of 29 days was higher for females in comparison to males in Bhils, while it was quite reverse for Minas, but difference was very narrow. The post-natal death was higher for females in both the tribes.

TABLE 10.3
INFANT AND CHILD MORTALITY BY AGE AND SEX

Age at death	Bhil			Mina		
	No. & % of male deaths	No. & % of female deaths	Total	No. & % of male deaths	No. and % of female deaths	Total
29 days and less	12 (26.09)	14 (29.17)	26 (27.66)	14 (25.45)	13 (25.00)	27 (25.23)
One month to 1 year	18 (39.13)	20 (41.67)	38 (40.43)	23 (41.82)	22 (42.31)	45 (42.06)
1-4 year	16 (34.78)	14 (29.16)	30 (31.91)	18 (32.73)	17 (32.69)	35 (32.71)
Total	46 (100)	48 (100)	94 (100)	55 (100)	52 (100)	107 (100)

It shows that up to the age of one year period, death of female infants were higher as compared to death of male infants in Bhils and Minas. The mortality in between the age of 1-4 years, higher for males than those in females in both the tribes, difference in percentage of male and female mortality in ages of up to 4 years was more significant in Bhils as compared to Minas.

SANITATION AND HYGIENE

Sanitation among Tribals are very poor. The houses are built of mud walls with thatched roofs devoid of proper ventilation. An enclosure for the animals is made within the household premises which leads to poor environment sanitation. There tribals depend on ponds, ditches, well and rivers for the source of drinking water. As a taboo, they do not take water from the hand pumps which have been erected by the governmental agencies. However, in some areas they do use these pumps as the source of drinking water.

Personal hygiene is also quite poor among the tribal groups. It can be attributed to the availability of water resources and poor awareness about the importance of personal hygiene.

Poor environment, sanitation and hygiene, therefore, result in the prevalence of various communicable and infectious diseases. Malaria is endemic in the tribal area and a considerable number of cases of diarrhoea, respiratory infections, venereal diseases, tuberculosis, skin diseases, vitamin deficiency and malnutrition have been seen among the tribal population groups. The morbid conditions carry tremendous risk to the infant and child mortality profile among these populations and there is an immediate need to evert this risk before it is accumulated in dangerous proportions.

INFANT FEEDING PRACTICES

In the tribes, traditionally breast milk has been the main source of nutrition to infants and even to children up to two years of age. Breast milk provides the child not only with necessary nutrition leading to better health due to naturally hygienic feeding but also immunizes him/her against certain infections. Proper infant feeding practices expect that the first breast milk should not be squeezed out from the breast but should be given to the child as it contains colostrum which provides natural immunity to the child. Further, the child should be given some supplementary foods like fluids or semi-liquids besides continuing breast milk from the fourth month onwards. When the child is around six months of age breast milk should become secondary and solid foods should form the main source of diet for the child. On the other hand, if the child is exclusively given breast milk for a prolonged period, it would not only be detrimental to the child's health but to the mother's health as well.

TABLE 10.4
PER CENT DISTRIBUTION OF LAST BORN, LIVING CHILDREN AGED 0-12 MONTHS BY BREAST FEEDING STATUS, FOOD SUPPLEMENTATION AND USE OF A BOTTLE WITH A NIPPLE ACCORDING TO AGE

Age of the child in months	Not Currently breast feeding	Breast milk only	Breast milk and			Total	Bottle-fed	No. of living children
			plain water	other liquid food	solid/ mushy			
0-3	2.6	64.9	18.6	13.4	0.4	100.0	7.4	231
4-6	2.7	41.5	26.6	27.1	2.1	100.0	9.0	188
7-9	3.4	23.0	21.3	40.2	12.1	100.0	8.6	174
10-12	6.0	17.0	20.0	30.0	27.0	100.0	5.0	100

To know the current situation with regard to the breastfeed and supplementation practices, a series of questions on relevant issues were asked to all respondents who delivered babies during four years preceding the survey.

The data reveals that about two third of the infant aged three months and below were found to be given exclusive breastfeed. This declined to 41 per cent for the age group 7-9 months. It is surprising that 17 per cent of mothers were giving exclusive breast feeding of children up to 12 months. Further Table 10.4 shows that in addition to breast milk, only few mothers reported to be giving other liquids like sugar solution, honey with water, outside milk, tinned milk, etc., in early infancy. Around 12 and 27 per cent of infants aged 7-9 months and 10-12 months respectively were given solid/mushy food.

CHILD REARING PRACTICES

Some other features which may affect fertility and mortality conditions are the prevailing conditions of carrying mother and child care. Right from the inception of a frequency to its termination, no specific diet is consumed by a woman. Inoculation against tetanus, iron, calcium and other vitamin intake is generally not observed by the expectant mother. More than 90 per cent of the deliveries are conducted at home attended by elderly ladies of household. Help of ANMs and LHVs is sought only in difficult labour. Similarly, post-delivery care is also very neglected. The concept of giving nutritious diet to mother after delivery is almost non-existent. All these factors contribute significantly to maternal mortality. Similarly, neonates and infants are the worst sufferers among these groups as far as child care is concerned. Poor sanitation, environment and personal hygiene which elevate the frequency of diseases like malaria, unspecified fevers, diarrhoea, respiratory diseases, meningitis, etc., take a heavy toll of children. Vaccination, immunization, drug therapies and followup have been found to be poor in these groups. Similarly, the breast-feeding infant in the first year does not receive any supplementary nutritious diet.

It can be said that poor health-seeking behaviour is the product of many factors interwoven among themselves like ignorance, superstitions, illiteracy, malnutrition, poor environment, sanitation and personal hygiene, availability of safe drinking water, unawareness of health education, living conditions, cultural lag, poorly developed mass media, poor medical and health opportunities and infrastructure on the administrative side contribute significantly to the morbidity, mortality and fertility conditions present among these tribal population groups.

REPRODUCTIVE HEALTH

The term reproductive health refers to a state of complete physical, mental and social well-being in all matters relating to the reproductive system and processes. It extends beyond the absence of disease and infirmity and therefore implies sexual health, i.e., the possibility of having a satisfying and safe sex life, the capability to reproduce and the freedom to decide if, when and how often to do so. Reproductive health services encompass the full range of methods and techniques required for that purpose. Reproductive health recognizes other individual needs, and not solely unmet contraceptive needs. It extends beyond the technical side of family planning, since it takes into account the factors affecting reproductive behaviour. These include the role of men, power relations between the sexes, the status of women, and the role of social institutions in reproductive strategies and individual choices. Implementation of the concept endeavours to integrate the viewpoint of women as persons with specific health needs.

India has among the highest maternal mortality rates known in the world. The recently completed National Family Health Survey reports the maternal mortality ratio for the country to be 420/100,000 live births, with 55/100,000 women of childbearing ages succumbing to maternal causes. According to the few community studies on maternal mortality, most of these deaths can be prevented through appropriate and timely intervention.

The study conducted in Rajasthan, shows that for every single maternal death, there were 23 episodes of morbidity, of which 9 were directly related to pregnancy and birth. According to study from Banswara District of Rajasthan, Scheduled Tribe poor women, during 1998, 27% of women who had at least one delivery had suffered from one or more serious problems related to pregnancy and child birth. While there were five maternal deaths and there were seven miscarriage. Further, study in Tribes showed that 78 per cent women had one or more gynecological problems, 87 per cent suffered from iron deficiency, anaemia and infections.

Anaemia during pregnancy is another widely prevalent problem. Banswara Tribal study found 87% of pregnant women to be anaemic (below llg/dl of hemoglobin). Of these, 62% were moderately anaemic and 27% were severely anaemic. The low-birth weight babies, or suffer miscarriages, still births or early child loss. Aanaemic woman is unable to cope with even a mild haemorrhage post partum, is at a greater risk of infections, and would take a longer time to recover from her vulnerable health condition.

The ideal number of children or the number desired is aimed at measuring the social norms that govern reproduction. Although highly correlated, the reproductive intentions of Triblal women are assessed in order to represent the individual's personal attitude toward the more short-term future, an approach with more predictive utility. Does she want to have another child soon or does she wish to postpone the next birth for some time? Or does she want no more children at all?

Tribal studies of Banswara shows (Nagda 1998) that the heavy load of reproductive morbidity among Triblal women is the outcome of their poverty, their powerlessness, low social status, malnutrition, infection, high fertility and lack of access to health care. Thus, socio-economic and biological determinants operate synergistically throughout the lives of poor women to undermine their health, resulting in high levels of morbidity and mortality. There is, therefore, an urgent need to design and implement services to address women's reproductive health needs.

FAMILY WELFARE SERVICES

Health development is compromised by rapid population growth, not only directly by the necessarily rapid quantitative expansion of health services but also indirectly by the retarding effects of sluggish economic development on improvements in housing and nutrition in particular. The factor of increasing population density can be seen itself on health. In spite of the fact that the introduction from public health programme like small pox and malaria eradication and water purification has brought about a very rapid decline in mortality. In tribal areas, 15000 population served by a doctor and 2500 persons estimated per bed. Whereas, for general population 11000 persons served per doctor and 1700 population served per bed. In tribal areas medical and health infrastructure is comparatively scarce. The situation is actually worse than the figures indicate because, deficiencies in modern equipment and medical suppliers mean that the effectiveness of a doctor or hospital is also less than the areas of total population. In the poorer tribals where disease rates and infant mortality are high, contagious and communicable diseases are rampant, malnutrition and under nourishment are woeful, illiteracy is exceedingly high, cultural and recreational activities are hardly organised.

PATTERN OF TREATMENT

Although there are Primary Health Centres and dispensaries in the block, the tribal people mainly depend for prevention and cure of their diseases on their traditional medicine men. Most of the tribal people rely for their treatment on their medicine men.

To a tribal mind, all fevers are alike and he hardly makes any difference between simple fever, typhoid fever, influenza, etc. Similarly he treats all stomach pains on the same footing whether it is dysentery pain or constipation or some other intestinal disorder. So far as diagnosis of the diseases is concerned, the tribal face a great difficulty particularly when they are confronted with any thing different from the common diseases. Most of the diseases are symptomatic. The name is generally given to some easily recognised and striking observed symptoms.

HEALTH STRATEGY FOR TRIBALS

In the tribes of Rajasthan, education standard is quite marginal. This situation becomes worst in case of female education. Unemployment, underemployment, malnutrition, diseases and poverty affected a very large number of tribal population. Medical facilities are just rudimentary. In tribal areas most posts of doctors are lying vacant the mortality rate was as high as 17.05 per 1000 whereas the figures for state was 13.2. The birth rate is quite higher (42.72 per 1000 population) among the tribals of Rajasthan. The infant mortality rate (IMR) is as high as 111 per 1000 live birth as compared to 96 in the state as a whole. In case of tribes, majority of children and mothers are facing malnutrition, resulting in decreased productivity.

The health conditions in tribal areas present an alarming situation and as such it is very difficult even today to provide satisfactory health care to the people. The main reasons attributed for the failure of the targets of programmes are:

1. Non-availability of medicines in most of the Health Centres.

2. Long distance between the villages and Health Centre.

3. Medical facilities provided in the blocks are not enough to check diseases such as TB, Leprosy and Ring Worm.

4. The family planning schemes has evoked little interest among the tribals due to the misconception, that the government is intent on destroying the tribal population.

5. Many health centres are not functioning due to lack of staff and inadequate finance. The number of medical institutions at present available is entirely inadequate to serve even minimum needs of the tribal people.

DEVELOPMENT AND EDUCATION

Rapid population growth impedes educational development in several ways. Most obviously it produces a rapid increase in the school age population. It also produces children dependency burden, forcing many students to drop out in order to work. The drop-out problem is more in tribal areas—it is estimated that about two-third of the students leave the school at the level of primary stage of education. The figures for total population was about 49 per cent. A large proportion of the poorer tribal children, on account of the rising cost of the schooling and economic burden cannot afford to benefit from them. Most tribals tend to use their children for ancillary services that would bring in some added income for their starving families.

In the state of Rajasthan during (1971 census) the percentage of literates and other educated persons among tribals in the urban areas was 19.67% and in the rural areas it was 6.18%.

LITERACY AMONG TRIBALS

Percentage of literacy among the tribal population in India for all persons was 8.53 per cent in 1961 and 16.31 per cent in 1981. In the case of males, it was 13.83 per cent in 1961 and 24.52 per cent in 1981 and for females, it was 3.16 per cent in 1961 and 8.04 per cent in 1981 census.

Whereas Rajasthan, has the lowest literacy rate except the state of Arunachal Pradesh in the country. Even the rate of growth of literacy in the state as compared with other states is not encouraging. In India, literacy increased to 12.21 per cent during the period 1961-81, whereas the same duration it increased to 9.17 per cent in Rajasthan. All India percentage increase of literacy for males and females has been almost equal: the position regarding the improvement of literacy rate of females as compared with males in Rajasthan has been much lesser.

The position of literacy among tribals of Rajasthan is extremely poor, and poorest in the case of female literacy. It is very painful and even disgusting to note that the literacy among tribals in Rajasthan increased to about 7 per cent during the period 1961-81 and the same period female literacy growth increased less than one per cent (Table 10.5). Almost total tribal female population in Rajasthan, continues to be illiterate. It becomes herculean or rather impossible task to effect any social and economic change among the tribals in face of mass prevailing illiteracy. However, there appears to be same improvement in 1991 while looking at female literacy rate in two tribal dominat districts—Banswara and Dungarpur which was about 16 and 12 per cent respectively.

TABLE 10.5
PERCENTAGE OF LITERACY IN TRIBAL POPULATION BY SEX IN RAJASTHAN FROM 1961 TO 1981

S.No.	*Years*	*Tribal Population*		
		P	*M*	*F*
1.	1961	03.98	07.42	0.28
2.	1971	06.46	12.02	0.20
3.	1981	10.27	18.85	1.20

WORKING FORCE

If population growth rate is substantially higher than the economic growth of the community, all the advances made would be swallowed in the growing stream of human masses. Fertility reductions could bring about a better sharing of income by fewer persons. The productive capacity of the economy is a function of the amount of natural resources, the accumulation of capital, and the quantity and quality of the labour force. In Scheduled Tribes, the working force participation rate for both male and female was higher than the total population.

RELEVANT ISSUES

Some of the issues related to the nature of tribal population and their development which need attention are as follows.

1. The tribal sub-plan approach was intended to narrow the gap between the levels of development of tribal and other areas has geared up the pace of development in the tribal area, yet it has not shown its impact on improving the quality of life, especially in terms of the level of literacy, health conditions, infant mortality,

mortality and status of women. However, the population growth rate in tribal areas is slightly declining.

2. Population of school age children is increasing. It has increased children dependency burdens, forcing many students to dropout in order to work. The drop-out problem is severe in tribal areas and needs attention.

3. Majority of people educated among the tribes of Rajasthan are Minas. There is a great need to pay attention on the less benefited other groups of tribal people.

4. In Rajashtan, literacy among the women has been comparatively lower than males needs attention.

5. In Scheduled Tribes, working force participation of female has been higher than the female participation in general population of Rajasthan. When tribal women are considered mainly as Labourers the quantitative improvement in their life is affected.

6. The coverage of health facilities in tribal areas is comparatively less, especially in terms of population-doctor ratio and number of hospital beds. Health functionaries find it difficult to reach remote areas with limited facilities at their disposal.

INTEGRATED STRATEGY

Although there are various factors for the under development and dehumanization, four factors, i.e., illiteracy, poverty, illhealth and civic inertia are the major significant factors. In order to tackle them, a four fold integrated strategy which incorporates education, employment, health and wealth organisation should be applied. In the ultimate analysis the administrative structure can be used to promote the urges and aspirations of the people. The motivation should be to propel the development administration to move in certain directions. Fortunately, in tribals areas, there has been a strong tradition of local representative bodies charged with important decision making. Tribal people has viable instruments of self rule anu self management. Our failure to make use of this instrument could be one reason for the tardy socio-economic progress both traditional and elective bodies. We should be able to reach down to the gross routes to make use of them. In other worlds, we should not confine ourselves merely to the higher echelons. The tribal sub-plan programmes can become vibrant and popular, if the traditional and elected bodies at various echelons of plan formulation and implementation co-operate with each other.

REFERENCES

1. L. Mukhopadhya and Others : Social Welfare. Vol XXXVI, No. 3-4. June-July 1989, New Delhi.
2. Social Welfare, *Ibid.*
3. Census of India, 1981, Series, India Part II B (i) XX, iii.
4. Census of India, 1991 Provisional Population totals, Rajasthan series 18.
5. *Ibid.*, 4.
6. Nagda, B.L. 1992, Social Correlates of fertility, Himanshu Publication, Udaipur.
7. Nagda, B.L. 1998, Quality Care and Client Satisfaction, A Study of Tribal District of Banswara District, PRC, MLS University, Udaipur.
8. Statistics of Children in India, Pocket Book 1990.
9. Bedi, M.S. 1988, Drinking Behaviour and Development in Tribal Areas, Udaipur.
10. *Ibid.*, p. 80.
11. Census of India 1991. *Op cit.*
12. Bedi, *Op cit.* p. 80.

11

A Study of Problems and Conditions of Rubber Plantation Workers in India

(With Special Reference To Arasu Rubber Corporation Ltd.)

Dr. M. Zathik Ali

Of all the factors of production, labour is the most important and major factor. This unavoidable factor plays a strategic role in production. The success and development of industrial sector depends to a larger extent upon the prosperity and growth of the workers. In fact, workers are human beings capable of holding responsibilities, extending co-operation and achieving industrial goals. Proper handling of labour leads to the success of industrial or other work and development of the country. Keeping in view the importance of labour, the state agencies, social welfare organisations, planners, employers, economists and others evince keen interest in studying the problems and conditions of labour. In this paper an attempt has been made to study the problems and conditions of Indian rubber plantation workers with special reference to Arasu Rubber Corporation Ltd.

* *Dr. Ali belongs to the Department of Economics, Mazharul Uloom College, Ambur - 635 802.*

This study is based on secondary data collected from various sources such as books, journals, reports of various private and government agencies, materials relating to Arasu Rubber Corporation Ltd. (ARCL) are collected from officials of the ARCL, Vadasery, Office of the Inspector of Plantation, Nagercoil, Trade Union leaders, workers and knowledgeable persons. The author has also made frequent visits to the rubber divisions for the purpose of cross verification and checkings. Personal observation has also helped a lot in writing this article.

INDIAN SCENARIO

Recruitment

During the initial period of rubber planting, difficulties were experienced by the rubber planters in securing required number of workers. Kankani system was followed to recruit workers for the rubber plantations. The workers who were drawn generally from the ranks of workers themselves are called Kankanis. The Kankanis -agents-middlemen—the maistries—were recruited by the planters in order to recruit labourers. The Kankanis were given money by the planters who, in turn, gave advance to the workers to attract them. The Kankanis were paid not only for bringing the labourers to the rubber plantations but also for their supervisory work. The system of advance to the workers was followed to induce them to agree to work in unknown forest areas 25 to 30 miles in the interior. There were two reasons for giving advance to the workers. Firstly, the workers were very poor and they left their family members behind. They needed food on their journey of two or three days. Therefore, they had to be paid advance. Secondly, advance was given "to bind down the labourer to his word". After appointment, the Kankanis received commission on the wages of the workers and maintained contact with them also. As a portion of wages was taken away by the Kankanis as Commission, the workers never received the full wage as a result of which the workers fell a prey to heavy debts.

In 1951 the Ministry of Labour, Government of India laid down certain criteria for eliminating the abuses of the Kankani system and gradual abolition of this system. The process of abolition of Kankani system commenced in 1951 and it was said to be completed in the then Madras State with the signing of the Valpari Agreement in the same year itself. On the other hand it was continued to be practised in

Kerala for sometime and abolished in 1962.[1] The difficulty regarding recruitment of the workers has now been solved.[2]

After abolishing the Kankani system of recruitment, the planters are using two sources, within and outside to recruit the workers. Recruitment of workers from outside may involve any one or more of the following methods. Selecting candidates, calling applications by advertisement, recruitment through employment exchange, scouting for talents in schools and colleges, and recruitment through agencies. The sources within plantations are nomination by present employers and trade unions. The purpose of selection is to find the best candidates from the applicants. Important methods of selections are interviews, tests, references and physical examinations. Factors such as education and training, skill, experience and physical characteristics are taken into consideration for selection.

Classification of Workers

On the basis of the main occupation, the workers in rubber plantations can be classified as (i) Tapper, (ii) Field Worker, (iii) Factory Worker and (iv) Watchman.

In any rubber estate field workers are appointed first. So, they used to be more in number than their counterparts. On some rubber plantations, the tapper are found to be more in strength. Table 11.1 gives an idea about the percentage distribution of different categories of workers in rubber plantation.

TABLE 11.1
PERCENTAGE DISTRIBUTION OF DIFFERENT CATEGORIES OF WORKERS IN RUBBER PLANTATION

S.No.	*Category of Workers*	*Number in Percentage*
1.	Tapper	45.00
2.	Field Worker	46.00
3.	Factory Worker	7.00
4.	Watchman	2.00
	Total	100.00

Source: The Rubber Board, Labour Welfare Schemes of the Rubber Board, Kottayam, 1988.

The rubber plantation workers are also classified into three categories as permanent, temporary and casual. In some estates contract workers are also found. Generally, the share of permanent, temporary and casual workers are 86 per cent, 10 per cent and 4 per cent respectively. Now-a-days the system of casual labour is abolished but the system of temporary worker is in existence.[3]

HOURS OF WORK

Before the implementation of the Minimum Wage Act in 1948, the hours of work vary from region to region, and estate to estate. No uniform rule was followed regarding hours of work. The workers were asked to work for more hours and women were forced to work in night shift also. The workers as a whole were extracted more work. The Minimum Wage Act regularised the hours of work. The perimissible hours of work according to the Minimum Wage Act, for adults in rubber plantations were nine hours a day and 48 hours in a week. The prescribed hours of work for children were 4½ hours a day.

The Central Wage Board for rubber plantation industry appointed in 1961 also considered the hours of work for the workers. Due to the nature of work in rubber plantations and the conditions prevailing in them, it was not possible to adopt the prescribed hours of work. The field workers who were employed on time rate basis were also to complete the work within 5 to 7 hours. But, the factory workers had to work for not less than 8 hours a day. Hence, the Central Wage Board fixed 8 hours of work a day for the time rated workers such as field workers and factory workers.

The Plantation Labour Act 1951 has also prescribed hours of work for the workers. According to Section 19(1) of the Plantation Labour Act, no adult worker shall be required or allowed to work on any plantation in excess of forty-eight hours a week. In other words, workers should not be required to work in a rubber plantation for more than 8 hours in a day.[4]

Wage Structure

The rubber plantation industry has long tradition of wage fixation through various methods like statutory minimum wage, negotiated settlement and tripartite discussion, etc. In the pre-independence period labour was wholly unorganised and wages in rubber plantation industry were very low. The workers as a whole were exploited by the planters. Wages were unilaterally fixed and the workers had no say in wage fixation. There was no standardisation of wage rates in the rubber plantation industry. Wages differed widely not only from region to region but also amongst the estates in the same region itself. Sex wage differential was a common feature.

After the enactment of the minimum wages, wages were fixed in the early fifties in various states. These states continued to be revised by revision of minimum wage as also in certain cases the issue of wage was referred to the Industrial Tribunal or Tripartite Committee through collective bargaining until the wage Board was constituted. Apparent wage revisions in the rubber plantation industry is made through negotiation and settlement between the parties concerned. However, the plantation industry is also in the schedule of the Minimum Wages Act 1948 and revision in the statutory Minimum wages are made as and when necessary.

In Kerala State wage rate in rubber plantation industry, in some cases, is still governed by the Minimum Wage Act 1948. In South India both time rated wages and piece rated wages are prevailing.

Minimum Wage Act 1948

During the Pre-independence period, there was no wage legislation to safeguard the interest of the rubber plantation workers. There were cases of exploitation, oppression, repression and so on. The attainment of independence in 1947 started a new era in the Indian history of labour movement. Our constitution gave due priority to the principle of socio-economic justice. As an instrument of wage regulation the Minimum Wage Act was passed by the Central Legislature in India in 1948. The Minimum Wage Act, 1948 applied to rubber plantation industry also.

The Minimum Wage Committee recommended minimum piece rate for field worker and factory worker. The Committee had also recommended fall back wages for the days on which the rubber plantation labourers are likely to be involuntarily unemployed. Table

11.2 gives the information regarding minimum wages recommended for the workers employed in rubber plantation industry.

TABLE 11.2
WAGES RECOMMENDED BY THE MINIMUM WAGE COMMITTEE

Sl.No.	*Categories of workers*	*Minimum wages in Rupees*		
1.	Field worker	Basic	D.A.	Total
	(a) Man	0.93	0.75	1.68
	(b) Woman	0.70	0.58	1.28
	(c) Child	0.46	0.37	0.83
2.	Factory workers			
	(a) Man	1.06	0.84	1.90
	(b) Woman	0.81	0.64	1.45

Source: Zathik Ali, M., A study of working and living conditions of Labour in Rubber Plantations in Kanyakumari district, Ph.D. thesis, Agra University, 1996.

Table 11.2 reveals that the wages have two components. They are basic wages and dearness allowance. The workers are classified into three types such as man, woman and child. The minimum wages recommended for factory worker is higher than that for the field worker. Sex wage differential is also evident from Table 11.2 and children are also employed. In the case of fall back wages also (Table 11.3) sex differential is shown.

TABLE 11.3
FALL BACK WAGES RECOMMENDED BY MINIMUM WAGES COMMITTEE

Sl.No.	*Categories of workers*	*Wages in Rupees*
1.	Man	0.85
2.	Woman	0.65
3	Child	0.45

Source: *Ibid.*

Central Wage Board for Rubber Plantation Workers

As in the case of other industries in rubber plantation industry also the Ministry of Labour and Employment, Government of India constituted a Central Wage Board in 1961. Soon after the constitution, the question of granting interim relief came up before the Wage Board for consideration. The Wage Board made certain recommendation which were accepted by the Government of India. Table 11.4 gives details regarding interim relief recommended by the Wage Board.

TABLE 11.4
INTERIM RELIEF RECOMMENDED BY THE CENTRAL WAGE BOARD.

Sl.No.	*Categories of workers*	*Interim relief in rupees*
I	Old workers	
	(a) Field workers	
	(i) man	0.15
	(ii) Woman	0.11
	(iii) Adolescent	0.09
	(iv) Child	0.08
II	New Workers	
	(a) Field and Factory workers	
	(i) Man	0.15
	(ii) Woman	0.11
	(iii) Adolescent	0.09
	(iv) Child	0.08

Source: Compiled from the Report of the Central Wage Board for the Rubber Plantation Industry.

As per Table 11.4 the workers are classified as man, woman, adolescent and child and different amount of interim relief was recommended for these categories of workers.

The final report was submitted by the Central Wage Board in August 1966. Table 11.5 provides information regarding wages recommended by the Central Wage Board for the workers in rubber plantation industry.

TABLE 11.5
RECOMMENDED WAGES BY THE FIRST CENTRAL WAGE BOARD FOR RUBBER PLANTATION INDUSTRY

S.No.	Categories of workers	With effect from				
		1.5.64	1.4.65	1.4.66	1.4.67	1.4.68
1.	Tapper	1.04	1.11	1.15	1.18	1.22
2.	Field worker	2.10	2.20	2.25	2.30	2.35
3.	Factory worker		2.30	2.40	2.45	2.50
2.55						

Source: Complied and calculated from the Report of the Central Wage Board for Rubber Plantation Industry.

Table 11.5 indicates that the Central Wage Board recommended lower wages for tappers and higher wages for factory workers. No further wage boards were constituted for rubber plantation industry. Subsequent wage revisions had taken place as a result of settlement through collective bargaining.[5] It cannot be denied that the wages settled through collective bargaining have improved wage rates but at the same time it can not be forgotten that the wages paid to the workers are lower than their counterparts in other organised industries.

Generally, job evaluation is the method followed in rubber plantation industry to determine the wages. The fact behind such evaluation is to find out what a job is worth. Ranking and classification systems are being adopted in determining the wages for the labourers.

Labour Welfare and Social Security Schemes

The Welfare activities in rubber plantations during the initial period of rubber planting were very meagre. Facilities such as canteen and creches were practically nil in rubber plantations. The estates situated in different parts of the country never cared to provide welfare facilities to the workers. In fact Social Security Schemes to rubber plantations workers were quite insignificant till 1947.[6] Though the Workmen's Compensation Act 1923 is applicable to the rubber plantations it did not give any substantial benefit to workers as accidents in rubber plantation were few. The Payment of Wages Act 1936, though applied to rubber plantations, was not comprehensive. In 1946, the Labour Investigation Committee observed that the conditions of life and employment in plantations were different from those employed in other industries. Therefore, the Investigation Committee recommended the creation of a plantation code covering all plantation areas. The Plantation Labour Act 1951 was thus enacted in the lines recommended by the Labour Investigation Committee.

The benefits and facilities provided under the Plantation Labour Act, 1951 include drinking water, latrine, medical, canteen, creche, recreation, education, housing accommodation, umbrellas, blankets, rain coats, weekly holidays and sickness and maternity benefits. But the benefits and facilities by the Plantation Labour Act 1951 did not seem to have reached the workers due to lack of proper implementation. The rubber planters seemed to have adopted various unlawful methods. The estates have been divided into several small holdings and workers were employed on contract basis. Temporary workers were also employed. As a result of indifferent attitude and approach of the planters, the Act was forced to be amended. By the 1981 amendment the coverage of the legislation has been enlarged and now it applies to any plantation admeasuring 5 hectares and employing 15 workers on any day in a year. Yet, a large number of rubber plantation workers are not covered by the Plantation Labour Act of 1951 because the average size of the rubber plantations in India is only 1.5 hectares.

Social Security Schemes

The following social Security Acts are applicable to the rubber plantation workers.

(i) Industrial Disputes Act, 1947

Industrial Disputes Act was passed in 1947. The Act deals with lay-offs, dismissals and retrenchment. According to this Act the following are the authorities for the settlement of disputes. (i) Works Committee, (ii) Conciliation officers, (iii) Board of Conciliation, (iv) Courts of Enquiry, (v) Labour Courts, (vi) Industrial Tribunals, (vii) National Tribunals, and (viii) Arbitration.

(ii) The Workmens Compensation Act, 1923

This Act was passed in March, 1923 and was put into force on Ist July 1924. This Act was amended in 1926 with the aim of introducing certain changes. Again it was amended in 1932 in the light of the recommendations made by the Royal Commission on Labour in India. After 1932, this Act underwent many changes for extending its scope and making the measures more effective and useful. The aim of this Act is to compensate the workers for the loss arising out of occupational diseases and industrial accidents.

(iii) Payment of Wages Act, 1936

The goal of this Act is to ensure regularity in payment to the workers and to prevent illegal and unauthorised deductions, etc.

(iv) Industrial Employment (Standing Orders) Act, 1946

"The Act requires the employer to define conditions of employment and to make such conditions as uniform as possible. For the purpose, standing orders are to be framed in all industrial establishments including plantations employing 100 or more persons. According to the scheme of the Act, draft standing orders are to be submitted to the certifying officer appointed by the State Government who is empowered to modify them so as to render the orders certifiable under the Act. Such certified standing orders are subject to review of an Appellate Authority in case of dispute. The authority also is appointed by the State Government. The draft standing order must be in conformity with the model standing order prescribed under the Act. The standing order framed under the Act after certificate have the force of law."

(v) The Minimum Wages Act, 1948

The Minimum Wages Act was enacted in March 1948. This Act is a landmark in the annals of Labour Legislation in India. The very aim of passing this Act is to prevent exploitation of labour through the payment of lower wages. This Act is meant to ensure the payment of Minimum Wages to the workers.

(vi) Factories Act, 1948

This Act came into existence in 1948. This Act also applies to the factory workers in rubber plantations to provide the worker with proper conditions of work.

(vii) Employees Provident Fund Act, 1952

This Act was extended to the rubber plantation workers in May 1957. The rate of contribution towards this fund was fixed at 6.25% at the time of the enactment of this Act. In 1965, it was enhanced to 8% in respect of estates employing fifty or more labourers.[7] The purpose of this Act is to provide against insecurity owing to natural factors such as old age, invalidity and death of the bread winners, etc.

(viii) Payment of Bonus Act, 1965

This Act was passed in 1965. This Act enables the workers to have a legitimate claim in the profit that a estate makes. Even if the establishment would incur a loss, it should pay a minimum bonus.

(ix) Payment of Gratuity Act, 1972

This Act applied to rubber plantation to which the Plantation Labour Act applies. The Act provides for a scheme of compulsory payment of gratuity to the employees.

(x) Equal Remuneration Act, 1976

This Act was passed with the laudable aim of paying equal remuneration for both men and women workers for the same work.

Apart from the above mentioned acts, the Rubber Board introduced four schemes in 1988 for the benefits of workers employed in small holdings who do not come under Plantation Labour Act, 1951.[8]

(xi) Educational Stipend Scheme

Under this scheme stipend is given to students closely related to the workers to purchase books, instruments and pay school or college fees.

(xii) Medical Attendance Scheme

Medical reimbursement benefits is given to the workers who have undergone treatment for illness exceeding two weeks in duration under this scheme.

(xiii) Housing Subsidy Scheme

Workers whose wage do not exceed Rs. 1600 per month are given Rs. 500 for finalising works like plastering, flooring. wiring, pumping and painting under this scheme.

(xiv) Group Insurance Cum Deposit Scheme

The aim of this scheme is to develop the habit of the workers to save on a long term basis and to cover their risk against accidents.

The above analysis reveals that the Government of India has enacted many Labour Acts for the welfare of the rubber plantation workers. But the implementation of these Acts in rubber plantations is a big question mark. No doubt, Inspectors of Plantations are appointed to make periodical visits to the plantations. They have to assertain whether the provisions of the plantation Labour Act are being observed in the plantations. They are "empowered to prosecute, conduct or defend before a court any complaint or other proceedings arising out of this Act".[9] But the question is to what extent the Inspectors of Plantations help the workers in securing the benefits and facilities provided under various Labour Acts must be probed into.

Table 11.6 shows the amount spent by the Rubber Board on Labour Welfare Schemes. Table 11.6 reveals that the Rubber Board has taken keen interest in the Welfare of the rubber plantation worker except for a few years, the amount expended on labour welfare scheme shows an increasing trend. The amount expended on labour welfare in 1961-62 was Rs. 124 thousand and it rose to Rs. 2281 thousand in the year 1990-91 indicating an overall increase of 1739.52 per cent over a period of 3 decades.

TABLE 11.6
EXPENDITURE ON LABOUR WELFARE

Year	Amount (in 000 Rs.)
1961-62	124
1970-71	150
1980-81	489
1990-91	2281

Source: Indian Rubber Statistics, Volume 19, The Rubber Board, Kottayam, 1991.

Trade Unionism

Illiteracy coupled with rural background, the rubber plantation workers were very much reluctant to join trade unions in the initial period. They were quite ignorant about the bargaining power. They were very much afraid of their employers. Besides, the isolated location of the estates and employer's effort to prevent outsiders from contacting the workers were the major contributing factors for the slow growth of trade unions during the initial period of rubber planting.

The trade union movement in rubber plantations is of recent origin. The Rage Committee which reported on the conditions of Labour in Plantations was of the view that there were only two trade unions in rubber plantations in India in 1949. These trade unions were not able to attract more workers. Due to poor strength and financial position, they vanished in due course of time. The entry of political parties and the enactment of the Plantation Labour Act in 1951 were mainly responsible for the growth of Unionism in rubber plantations. The National Commission on Labour in its report in 1968 revealed that nearly 67% of the workers in rubber plantations were members of trade unions.[10] As per the latest indication, the strength of trade union membership has touched more than 90%.[11]

Though the trade unions have very strong root in rubber plantations, they have many defects. The obvious feature of the trade union is multiunionism due to the advent of outside leadership with full domination over trade unions. More than 90% of the trade union leaders are from outside belonging to some political parties with different ideologies. This is said to be the result of the weakness of Indian Labour Legislation which provides for the existence of more than one Union with outside leadership. It hinders the achievements of healthy goals of workers in the rubber plantations. Another notable cause of weakness of trade unions in rubber plantations is irregular subscription by workers. The common fund of the trade unions especially in Tamil Nadu and Karnataka is very small rather meagre. A serious defect found even at the present stage of development of trade unions in rubber plantations is mutual and internal differences and bickerings based on bias or caste considerations or political string. The employers at times do try to adopt some tricky means to disrupt the unity among the workers either by winning or alluring the leaders or creating fictions among the labourers and leaders of trade unions.

Despite the defects, it cannot be denied that the trade unions have been playing a pivotal role in bringing about hikes in wages and fighting continuously against the planters for the proper and earnest implementation of various Labour Welfare Measures for the benefits of the rubber plantation workers.

Women Workers[12]

Traditionally rubber plantations have been employing large number of women workers. According to the Labour Investigation Committee, about 25% of total labour force in rubber plantations were women workers. Heavy work load is an important problem of the women workers in rubber plantations. They are employed generally on a piece-rate basis and recruitment is on family basis. Women workers are preferred to unskilled works. They are generally not given job training facilities. Lower wages are given to them. The unequal wages for women still continues in some parts of states such as Tamil Nadu despite the legislation for Equal Remuneration Act passed in 1976. The wages of women workers are not lesser than men but also far below the statutory rate. In certain areas women workers have to cover the distance of about 170 to 525 metres to fetch drinking water from the rivers, tanks, streams and canals. They do not have their own houses.

The creches in the gardens are found to be below the prescribed standard of constructions. They are not being maintained in clean and good sanitary conditions. In this connection it is worthwhile to quote the statement made by the Union Labour Ministry. Government of India, "the maintenance of creches was quite poor, particularly in the small estates of Tamil Nadu and Karnataka. Children were not found to be wearing uniforms, but were in dirty clothes...creche attendants do not care to use them. The mother also complained that these creches were being washed once in a week". In Kerala, Tamil Nadu and Karnataka schooling facility is not provided beyond primary level. "It is an established fact that married women are denied employment to avoid the obligation of paying maternity benefit or creche for their children." In reality, the legislation concerning women workers are not implemented. In short, "lack of education and civic consciousness, underemployment and poverty and other drawbacks continue to present in the life of women workers employed in plantations".

Child Labour

Children are the blooming flowers of the society. It becomes the duty of the society to protect the children from the damaging effects. But in contrast, child labour constitutes an important fraction of the total labour force. Child labour was found even in ancient days. Even today the children are compelled to labour for others simply for their existence. The child labour is supplied by contractors. They are employed to assist their parents at work. Poverty forced the children to go for work. Taking it as an advantage, the employers exploit the situation by appointing child labour with low wages that also endorses the statement of Davis who observes that child labour exists not because children are more able workers but because they can be had for less money.

The employment of children is considerable in rubber plantations which is not shown on record generally by the planters for obvious reasons. But the Government is well aware about this when the report of the Working and Living conditions of Plantation Labour in South India said "however, it was informally gathered that employment of children still continues".

PROFILE OF ARASU RUBBER CORPORATION LTD. (ARCL)

Arasu Rubber Corporation Ltd., (ARCL) in Kanyakumari District, has 8 rubber divisions and 2 rubber factories under its control. Total area under rubber is 4787 hectares and the total tapping area is 3196 hectares. Total production which stood at 2300 metric tonnes in 1985-'86 has increased to 2900 metric tonnes in 1994-'95 indicating an overall increase of 26.09%. The revenue of this corporation over a period of one decade has increased from 292.37 lakhs in 1985-'86 to 855.54 lakhs in 1994-'95. The increase in revenue is computed to be 192.62%. This corporation provides employment to 2562 workers of which 48.39% are tappers, 11.63% are relief tappers, 34.43% are field workers and 5.46% are factory workers. Keeripari is the rubber division where maximum (12.02%) workers are employed and minimum (0.94%) workers are employed in Mylar rubber factory.

Recruitment of Workers

Before the establishment of ARCL, advertisement and Employment Exchange were used as sources of labour supply. Usually the then General Manager of the Government rubber plantations called for candidates through advertisement in newspapers whenever there were vacancies in any Government rubber plantations. Those candidates who responded to the advertisement were asked to attend an interview. A committee under the Chairmanship of the Divisional Forest Officer concerned was constituted to recruit workers, to rubber plantations where vacancies existed. The workers were also recruited through the Employment Exchange at Nagercoil.[13]

After the establishment of ARCL, the system of recruitment through advertisement was stopped in 1985 and the Employment Exchange is the only source of labour supply. Under the system of recruitment through Employment Exchange a committee under the Chairmanship of the Managing Director is constituted to recruit the required number of workers. The Managing Director is assisted by a team of officials in recruiting suitable workers. The candidates who are sent by the Employment Exchange are interviewed. On the basis of their performance they are recruited. For the tapping work, the candidates are taken to the plantation and asked to tap the rubber tree. On the basis of their skill in tapping, the workers are recruited. Dependents of the deceased workers who die before their retirement are given preference in recruitment.[14]

Number of Working Days

Like their counterparts in agriculture sector, the workers in ARCL are not given work throughout a year. Three factors can be attributed for this sorry state of affair. They are (1) Rest period (2) Rainy days and (3) week-end holidays.

(1) *Rest Period*: Rest period refers to a period of time during which leaf fall occurs. The duration of rest period in a year is normally one month. Generally it starts from the last week of February and ends in the last week of March. As tapping is not possible during the rest period, the workers are not given work which affects the working days.

(2) *Rainy-days*: Since no work can be performed during rainy days in rubber plantations, all categories of workers remain idle. Generally, rainy days effect 45 working days in a year. Working days vary with changes in number of rainy days.

(3) *Week-end holidays*: As per section 20 of Plantation Labour Act, 1951, every worker should be provided a day of rest for every period of seven days. But no provision is made in the Act to pay wages during holidays. Week-end holiday is given on every Sunday. Table 11.7 provides information regarding availability of employment to the workers in ARCL taking the above three factors into consideration.

TABLE 11.7
AVAILABILITY OF EMPLOYMENT (DAYS PER YEAR)

S.No.	*Particulars*	*No. of days*	*Percentage to the Total*
1.	Working days	240	65.75
2.	Idle days	125	34.25
Total		365	100.00

Source: As in Table 2

Table 11.8 gives an idea about the working hours in rubber division.

TABLE 11.8
DISTRIBUTION OF WORKING HOURS

S.No.	*Categories of workers*	*Working hours*	*Interval*
1.	Tappers	Hours from 6 A.M.to 2 P.M.	No interval
2.	Field workers	8 hours from 6 A.M. to 12.30 P.M. and from 1.30 P.M. to 4.30 P.M.	1/2/ hour from 12.30 P.M. to 1.30 P.M.
3.	Factory workers	-do-	-do-

Source: As in Table 11.2.

Since the tappers are paid piece rate wages, they generally do not take more than six hours a day to complete the tapping work.

They also do not take any interval for taking food. As soon as the work is over the tappers used to leave the estates.

Leave and Holidays with Wages

Workers in other industries are entitled to avail themselves of various types of leaves such as casual leave, Earned leave, Privilege leave, Medical leave, leave with half pay, special leave etc. But the workers in ARCL are allowed only earned leave which is the only leave benefit to the workers. The women workers are given maternity leave in addition to the earned leave. Table 11.9 gives the information with regard to leaves and holidays in ARCL.

TABLE 11.9
LEAVES AND HOLIDAYS

S.No.	*Particulars*	*No.of days/weeks*
1.	Earned leave	1day for every 20 working days
2.	Maternity leave	6 weeks
3.	National and Festival holidays	9 days

Source: As in Table 11.2.

Table 11.9 reveals the following facts:

1. Workers in ARCL are not allowed leaves such as casual leave, privilege leave, special leave, etc.
2. Earned leave is allowed as per rule, i.e., every employee is entitled to leave with full pay of one day for every 20 days of duty.
3. Maternity leave is allowed. Women workers are granted a total of 3 weeks leave with pay—three weeks before and 3 weeks after delivery.
4. Workers are allowed 9 national and festival holidays with wages in each calendar year.

Wages

Workers in ARCL are paid daily wages. Piece rated wages and time rated wages are in prevalent in ARCL. While tappers are paid piece rate wages, the other categories of workers, viz., field workers and factory workers are given time rate wages.

Under piece rate wage system each tapper is allotted two coupes from which latex is to be tapped on alternative days. Standard output is fixed according to the grade of the latex. There are four grades of latex. The standard output of grade IV latex is 8 kg out of which latex is 6.400 kg and scrap is 1.600 kg. Similarly, standard outputs of grade III latex, grade II latex and grade I latex are 6.500 kg, 4 kg and 2 kg respectively. The respective proportion between latex and scrap grades III, II and I are 5.200 : 1.300 kg, 3.200 : 0.800 kg and 1.600 : 0.400 kg. In addition to this standard output, for every additional one kilo of latex an additional remuneration of Rs. 1.10 is paid and for every additional one kilo of scrap, 50 paise is paid. A cut in wages is effected if the total output turned out by workers falls below the standard output. The cut in wages per kilo of grades IV, III, II and I latex are Rs. 0.90, Rs. 1.10, Rs. 1.80 and Rs. 2.50 respectively.

Wages in ARCL is not paid daily. On every Friday Rs. 120 is paid if the workers have worked for 6 days. The balance amount is paid in the next subsequent month between Ist and 10th day.

The wages have two components, viz: Basic and D.A. Basic wages are fixed on the basis of negotiated settlement between the management of ARCL and the trade unions once in every three years. D.A. is linked to 3434 points of average consumer price index for Nagercoil centre (1939=100). Further adjustment of D.A. is to be made from the level of 3434 points of consumer price index for Nagercoil centre. Rs. 1.60 is to be paid for every unit of 5 points increase. The adjustment is made on the Ist April, the Ist August and Ist December of each year on the four monthly average of the second previous four months period to the date of revision.[15]

The daily wages of workers in ARCL are presented in Table 11.10.

TABLE 11.10
DAILY WAGES OF WORKERS

S.No.	*Categories of workers*	*Basic wages (Rs.)*	*D.A. (Rs.)*	*Total Wages (Rs.)*
1.	Tapper	14.60	27.51	42.11
2.	Field worker	14.10	27.51	41.61
3.	Factory worker	15.45	27.51	42.96

Source: As in Table 11.2

Of all categories of workers factory workers are paid more wages though the difference is very insignificant. No discrimination in wages is shown between male and female workers. In other words, Equal Remuneration Act, is effectively implemented. The casual workers are also paid on par with permanent workers. In Table 11.11 average daily wages given to workers in ARCL for a period of 10 years from 1985 to 1994 is presented.

TABLE 11.11
AVERAGE DAILY WAGES

S.No.	Year	Average Daily	Percentage	Wage trend
1.	1985	22.61		19.588
2.	1986	23.18	2.52	21.868
3.	1987	24.30	4.83	24.178
4.	1988	25.13	3.42	26.488
5.	1989	26.93	7.16	28.798
6.	1990	27.80	3.23	31.108
7.	1991	29.14	4.82	33.418
8.	1992	36.53	25.36	35.728
9.	1993	41.22	12.84	38.038
10.	1994	42.69	3.57	40.348

Note: The equation of the straight line trend is
$Y = a + bx = 29.953 + 1.555\ x$

Source: As in Table 11.2

Table 11.11 reveals that there is an increase in average daily wages from year to year. This is due to the changes in the cost of living index. The percentage increase in daily wages fluctuates from year to year and touches the maximum in 1992 perhaps due to abnormal increase in the cost of living in the same year. The increase over a period of one decade from 1985 to 1994 is computed to be 88.81%.

Labour Welfare Measures[16]

The workers in ARCL are entitled to avail themselves of different benefits and facilities provided under Plantation Labour Act 1951, which was put into force from Ist April 1954 for the welfare of plantation workers only. The extent to which these benefits and facilities are made available to the workers are analysed below.

Drinking water facility is provided in all the divisions. Water is supplied from well. Tap connections have been given for the release and use of water stored in the manner prescribed. Conservancy facility is provided in all the divisions. All the urinals and latrine are provided with sufficient water and urinals are roofed. Latrines have septic tanks.

As far as medical facilities are concerned, group hospitals are not available. ARCL has two garden hospitals. Each garden hospital has a doctor. Dispensaries are available in the rest of the divisions. The doctors employed in the garden hospitals make periodical visits to the dispensaries on rotation basis. There is a general complaint about the availability of the required medicines in the dispensaries. Generally prescriptions are given by the visiting doctors and the workers are asked to buy the medicines from outside sources. The workers in one voice complained that no proper treatment is given to them. They also expressed the view that very ordinary cheap priced medicines are given. They further added that doctors are irregular in their visits and for surgical treatment they are forced to go to private hospitals. The workers are not paid any financial assistance for taking medical treatment from private hospitals. Though the management denied all the charges categorically, there is truth in the complaints lodged by the workers against the medical facility.

Canteen facility is available to the workers in ARCL. Coffee, tea and snacks are sold on profit basis. The canteens are not properly maintained. Creches are available to the worker's children in all divisions. Items such as milk, clothes, soap and oil are not supplied. But, these items are to be supplied as per the Act. All the rubber divisions in the ARCL are facilitated with the materials necessary for playing chess, volleyball and badminton. It is observed that televisions found at the common places are not properly used. Playgrounds are not maintained clearly. Films are rarely screened.

The ARCL has made available educational facilities to the children of workers from 3 primary and 2 middle schools of its own. For higher education, the children have been going to towns and nearby villages. Some of the workers have also sent their children to convents where the managements are collecting exorbitant fees from the parents. The workers have to pay huge amount towards the travelling expenses of their children getting education from outside sources.

So far the ARCL has constructed and provided 1478 houses to the workers. All houses have latrine and water facilities. These houses have cement flooring and each house is electrified. Those workers who have not been allotted houses are given house rent allowance of Rs. 25. While women workers in ARCL are given sickness and maternity benefit as per rule, all categories of workers are availing themselves of the weak-end holiday on every Sunday. Umbrellas and blankets are also provided to the workers.

Social Security Measures [17]

Minimum wages are paid to all categories of workers. Even casual workers are paid minimum wages. Provident fund benefit is available in ARCL. Each worker has to contribute 8% towards provident fund. In addition to the provident fund contribution the workers are also paying 2% towards family pension. Bonus is paid at the rate of 8.33% to the workers. In addition to this, an ex-gratia amount of Rs. 1000 is also paid to the workers.

The officials of ARCL claimed that compensation is paid to the workers involved in industrial accidents as per rules. But the trade union leaders have given a different picture. They regretted that the officials are very reluctant in paying compensation in the event of any worker involved in an industrial accident. The officials have the tendency to escape from paying compensation by using certain rules of the Workmen's Compensation Act 1923 to their favour. The workers are driven to approach the labour court through their unions for getting compensation as the officials are not voluntarily paying it. The workers who retire from their service are compensated by gratuity. The gratuity amount is paid to the retiring workers as per the rule laid down by Act.

Apart from the above mentioned welfare and social security benefits and facilities the workers are also benefited by the non-statutory welfare measure such as festival advance which is given to the workers to celebrate their religious festivals. Rs. 200 is paid to each worker so as to enable him to meet his additional expenditure in connection with celebrating the festival. The advance amount is to be returned in 10 equal instalments by the workers.

Strikes [18]

The workers in ARCL have so far organized four major strikes through their trade unions. Major unions such as CITU and INTUC have their wings in the rubber divisions. More than 90 per cent of the workers are the union members. The strikes were launched in 1969-'70, 1976-'77, 1981-'82 and 1990. The causes are varied and consequences are different. The causes and results of the strikes are shown in Table 11.12.

TABLE 11.12
CAUSES AND RESULTS OF STRIKES

S.No.	Year	Cause	Result
1.	1969-70	Permanency of workers, minimum of 240 working days.	Partially Successful
2.	1976-77	Dearness allowance	Partially Successful
3.	1981-82	Bonus and setting up of a Government Rubber Corporation	Successful
4.	1990	Monthly salary	Unsuccessful

Source : As in Table 11.2.

Before 1969-70 the workers were not given the status of permanent workers and thus were kept outside the purview of Welfare Acts such as Plantation Labour Act 1951. If they were made permanent they would become eligible to avail themselves of the benefits and facilities conferred by different Labour Welfare Acts. Representations from the workers were rejected and thrown in dust bin. The workers who lost their patience have become irritant and militant and decided to indulge in direct action. At the initial stage mild actions such as demonstration and dharna were initiated and as these measures did not yield expected results the workers were forced to launch an indefinite strike on November 1969 which came to an end on 6 May 1970. The workers also fought for a minimum of 240 working days. Having found no way other than coming to an agreement with the workers the management had accepted these two demands in principle and promised to implement them subsequently after the formalities were over. It is observed that there are still casual workers who are eligible to be made permanent. The workers are generally given 240 working days in a year but in some years the management is not able to engage the labourers with work for 240 days due to causes beyond its control and the outcome of this strike is partial successful.

Whatever may be the general level of prices, the workers in rubber divisions were paid only fixed DA which could in no way help the working class to meet their expenses. So attempts were made to get DA based on the cost of living index of Nagercoil centre before 1976. They could not but indulge in direct action and a strike was organised on 1.10.1976 which had lasted for 90 days. Finally, it was agreed by the management that an additional 3 paise would be paid for every five point increase in the cost of living index of Nagercoil town. This agreement was brought into operation from 1.1.77. The result of the strike is successful.

The workers were denied bonus on the plea that as they were the employees of government of Tamil Nadu, they were not eligible to avail themselves of the bonus benefit. This led to the workers to go on an indefinite strike which lasted for a longer period from 17.11.81 to 15.03.1982. As a result of the strike an adhoc measure was taken by the government, according to which an ex-gratia bonus at the rate of 26 working days per year was paid. Meanwhile, the workers had also fought for setting up of a government rubber corporation which was also established on 1.10.84. After the establishment of ARCL,the workers have been receiving bonus at the rate of 8.33 per cent. At present, in addition to the 8.33% bonus, an ex-gratia bonus of Rs. 1000 is also paid to the workers. The result of their strike can be regarded as successful.

Despite repeated requests and appeals by the workers and the unions, the authorities of ARCL have not considered the demand for the payment of monthly salary to ward off their sufferings. Consequently, a strike was started by the workers on 17th Oct. 1990. As this strike gathered momentum and intensified it was extended for a span of 65 days. As their demand has not yet seen the light of the day, it still continues to be the dream of the poor proletariat of ARCL.

NOTES AND REFERENCES

1. Government of India, National Commission on Labour, Report of the Study Group for Plantations (Coffee, Rubber) , Ministry of Labour, New Delhi, 1968, p. 15.
2. Bhogoliwal, T.N., Economics of Labour and Industrial Relations, Sahita Bhawan, Agra, 1990, p. 128.
3. The Rubber Board, Labour Welfare Schemes of Rubber Board, The Rubber Board, Kottayam, 1988, p. 131.
4. Zathik Ali, M., 'A Study of Working and Living Conditions of Labour in Rubber Plantations in Kanyakumari District, unpublished Ph.D. Thesis, Agra University, Agra, 1996, p. 130.
5. *Ibid.* , p. 143.
6. Government of India, Report on An Enquiry into Conditions of Labour in Plantations in India, 1946, p. 349.
7. Haridasan, V., Rubber Plantation Labour—Problems and Prospects, Rubber Planters Conference Souvenir, 1974, p. 76.
8. The Rubber Board, Labour Welfare Schemes of the Rubber Board, *op. cit.*, pp. 2-28.
9. Rule 3(11), Tamil Nadu Plantations Labour Rules, 1955.
10. National Commission on Labour, Report of the Study Group for Plantations (Coffee, Rubber) 1968, p. 25.
11. The Rubber Board, Labour Welfare Schemes of the Rubber Board, *op. cit.*, p. 1.
12. (a) Viswanath Gupta, "Women Workers in Tea Plantations", *Social Welfare*, Vol. XXXVII, No. 2, May 1990, p. 29.

    (b) Badruddin, "Women Workers in Assam Tea Plantations. *Social Welfare*, Vol. XXXVII, No. 2. May 1990, p. 29.

    (c) Government of India, "Occupational Health Issues of Women Workers in the Unorganised Sector", Report of the Task Force on Health, the National Commission of Self-Employed Women, the Department of Women and Child Development, Ministry of Human Resources Development, New Delhi, 1989, p. 71.
13. Interview with the Managing Director, ARCL, Vadasery.
14. Zathik Ali, *op. cit.*, p. 107.
15. Interviews with the Secretary CITU, Kulasekaram and the workers of ARCL.
16. Zathik Ali, *op. cit.*, pp. 164-77.
17. *Ibid.*, pp. 178-81.
18. Interviews with the Secretaries of different Trade Unions and the Workers of ARCL.